HUNTING NORTH-WOODS BUCKS

Eric - I hope you
enjoy the read. Thanks
for all the good times!

Hunting North-Woods Bucks

Lessons & Lore From The Northern Forests

Steve Heiting

For Connie
(again)

Special thanks to Dean Bortz, Kevin Schmidt, John Stellflue, Jordan Weeks and Ken Jackson for their input as this book was nearing completion, and to all of my hunting partners, past and present, for the good times we have shared.

Published by
Pinemere Press
An imprint of Steve Heiting Outdoors
PO Box 326, St. Germain, WI 54558
www.steveheiting.com

Printed in the U.S.A. by
ColorHouse Graphics, Grand Rapids, Michigan

ISBN: 978-0-9960579-1-2 (printed version)
ISBN: 978-0-9960579-2-9 (digital version)

HUNTING NORTHWOODS BUCKS

FOREWORD

In November of 1971, a 12-year-old kid growing up in Wisconsin's Ashland County learned a valuable lesson when it comes to hunting northwoods deer. "There's more out there that ain't a deer than is," said his grandfather about midway through his first Opening Day. His grandpa had just come back from making his second 1-man push of the day and they were still-hunting — or at least slowly walking and looking — as they headed past the Tank Hole on Bosner Creek to make another drive. As he walked, the kid rolled those words around in his head, left to come up with his own translation, since Grandpa never wasted words on explanations. It kind of sounded like he meant "don't get your hopes of shooting a buck up too doggone high, or you might be sorely disappointed."

If that's what he meant, then Grandpa was right. It took that kid nine years to shoot his first northwoods buck — a spiker that came through on a drive in the Log Creek area of Price County.

There is nothing easy about hunting whitetails anywhere. True enough. Hunting whitetails in the large tracts of forested land that make up what we call the "northwoods?" Those forests in the Great Lakes and northeastern states, and Canadian provinces? I don't think anyone would argue that the whitetail challenge ratchets up a notch or two in the northland. Here the logistics of putting together a safe hunt can be as much of a hurdle as hunting lower deer densities over a sprawling land base.

So, why bother then, you might ask? Well, because you have this book — *Hunting Northwoods Bucks* — in your hands, you're about to find out. In this book, Steve Heiting takes the reader through his more than 30 years of northwoods hunting experiences and, along the way, Steve shares with you his knowledge of hunting big bucks in big country. Many of you may associate Steve's name with musky fishing — and for good reason. Steve is the managing editor of *Musky Hunter* magazine and is co-owner of the University of Esox Musky Schools. Sure, he catches plenty of muskies each year, but I tell you what — this big rascal can hunt, too. That's going to be very apparent to you as you read his book.

I don't know just how long I've known Steve, but it's probably been a good 20 years at the time this book was published. For much of that time, we've lived in the same general area of northern Wisconsin that fits the northwoods definition. We've been trading hunting stories, game sighting updates, and more hunting stories for most of those years. We've fished together more often than we've hunted together, but in the spring of 2013 we did chase turkeys in a northwoods setting that was just as challenging as any big woods whitetail hunt. Now that I've read Steve's book, I can see that many of the principles that he applies to deer hunting also apply to his northwoods turkey hunting. A good game plan, a little bit of confidence, and a measure of persistence brought him face-to-face with a thundering triple-bearded gobbler that day.

Another thing that I noticed that day? Steve was comfortable in the big woods. That's one trait — or sense of being if you want to put it that way — a hunter has to have if he has any hope of being successful out there. And I'm not talking just about the fear of getting lost. That might have been the first consideration 20 years ago, but these days, with GPS units and cell phone apps, there's little chance anyone is going to get lost. The only way that's going to happen is if there is no cell coverage or the phone or GPS battery dies. But even with navigation no longer a major concern, I still see people who are not comfortable hunting in the big woods. In farm country, it's relatively easy to decide where to place a stand, or how to set up a drive because, in many cases, white-tailed deer travel routes are limited. Not so in the northwoods. Deer can travel anywhere they want. A hunter has to be comfortable in this big landscape in order to have the confidence needed to select a stand site, still-hunting route or to plan a drive.

I've seen Steve feeling mighty comfortable over the years on backwoods fishing expeditions where the mosquitoes were as big as sandhill cranes and twice as loud. Whether it was rowing a small northwoods river for hidden muskies, or bushwhacking our way into small musky lakes, didn't matter. Boots on, head down, let's go. By the way, if Steve ever asks you if you have a chainsaw, say no. The one time I said yes I ended up sawing fallen trees out of the tote road so we could reach a backwoods lake that held hungry muskies, but was guarded by those sandhill crane mosquitoes.

What you're going to find here is that Steve isn't going to tell you how to hunt deer in the northwoods, he tells you how he hunts those deer. What has worked for him, and his hunting partners. Steve's techniques and ideas may well work for you, too, but you are also welcome to adapt these ideas into your hunting style. What Steve's really doing here is inviting you into the northwoods if you have yet to hunt here, or to hunt the northwoods in a bit of a different way if you haven't had much luck so far. You're also going to hear some stories about hunting in the northwoods; some modern day, some from way back in the day. Those stories put some fabric on this thing we call northwoods deer hunting. In some ways, those stories are as much a part of hunting the northwoods as are the big-shouldered bucks that live here. With a little bit of confidence, a dash of persistence, a good plan and maybe even a little bit of luck, you'll be able to add a chapter to the story Steve has started here.

One of my best hunting partners, my cousin Duane — toward the end of every gun season after we had beaten every bush in three counties looking for deer — he would say, "Well boys, let's split up and take and mosey through the big country." Duane's no longer with us, but his words are and every year northwoods buck hunters live by them.

Boys, let's take and mosey through that big country one more time. Start right here.

— Dean Bortz, Editor
Wisconsin Outdoor News
April 2014

The author in 1984 with his first northwoods buck. The 202-pound animal was shot over two miles from the author's truck and required a 9-hour drag.

PREFACE: THE TRADITION RUNS DEEP

Deer hunting is my escape. It's my time to reconnect — with my primal urge to hunt, with the natural world, and with friends I may not have seen since the previous deer season. When I hunt, I know I will feel tired at day's end, sometimes I feel elated, often I feel frustrated, but most of all I feel satisfied. Few things do that for me and hunting deer in the northwoods is high on my list.

It may seem odd that I am such an enthusiastic hunter, given what I do. As managing editor of *Musky Hunter* magazine, I have a dream job. Who wouldn't want to make a living doing something that others do for fun? And shouldn't I be musky fishing rather than deer hunting in the fall months, since giant fish put on the feedbag prior to winter?

Yes, I'll admit, mine is one of those jobs that sometimes causes me to pinch myself during the drive to work to make sure I'm not dreaming. But with increasing intensity each fall, I eat, sleep and breathe deer hunting.

I saw the same thing happen to several other experienced, even big name, musky fishermen. There was a time I couldn't understand how they could fish hard through the summer but then back off in the fall months. Now I do.

Maybe as all serious musky anglers fully embrace catch-and-release fishing, hunting better fulfills some primal yearning buried within our psyche to return home with something tangible from our pursuits. We all understand that the future of musky fishing demands catch-and-release, so that should not change. Therefore, in the deepest recesses of our being, maybe we feel more fulfillment from a big buck lying in the back of a pick-up truck than a digital photo of a big musky we released.

And now I've taken my fall obsession a step further by writing a book about it. The fact is, I love to hunt deer in the northwoods but I can't find any books that address the subject. I've been hunting the northwoods exclusively for over three decades and try to read everything about deer hunting. I believe that if I pick up one idea from an article or a book, or I'm merely entertained, then the time and money spent were worthwhile. I can find bits and pieces of information that apply to northwoods deer hunting, but never a whole book. (The closest I've found to the subject are *Hunting Big Woods Bucks, Vols. 1 & 2*, by Maine guide Hal Blood. Both are excellent and highly recommended.)

Whether I'm qualified to write a book about northwoods deer hunting is up to you. There are certainly those who do better than me, especially when it comes to still-hunting and tracking. But I've killed bucks by every way imagineable, from stand-hunting to still-hunting to tracking to making drives, with rifles, bows and muzzleloaders. A nice collection of the bucks I've taken exceeded 200 pounds field-dressed, and I've driven some very big bucks to my hunting partners. I hope that is enough to qualify me to write these words.

My definition of the "northwoods" is the forested areas of the upper reaches of Wisconsin, Minnesota and Michigan in the Midwest, and northwest Ontario. While I have never hunted in the East, I hope some of this applies to upstate New York, northern Maine, and other northern parts of the whitetail's domain. The northwoods deer hunter demographic is miniscule compared to the hunters of more agricultural areas, but we are every bit as dedicated.

Outside of what I have picked up from my hunting partners, everything that I discuss in this book was learned the hard way — by myself. Even when I shot my first buck at the age of 17, I was the only one there when it was time to gut the thing and get it out of the woods. You see, I didn't start deer hunting until I was 16 years old, which is comparatively late for many but I had to wait until I was old enough to drive. My father had hunted when he was younger, but illness prevented him from taking me when I was of hunting age. My mother's father — an avid hunter — died when I was 10 years old, and my Grandpa Ben, my dad's father, was in failing health by the time I was old enough to hunt. Many of my earliest memories are of fishing with Grandpa Ben, and as a kid I tried to finagle as much time with him at his cabin in northern Wisconsin as I could. That's probably why I have a deep love for the northwoods — you never knew what a new day would bring, and the potential for adventure lay around every corner or over every hillside. Grandpa Ben's largest buck was a 9-pointer, and I still have the antlers.

It wasn't until I took a job in extreme northern Wisconsin in 1984 that I began hunting the North, where I quickly learned that the deer hunting tradition runs deep. I also found miles upon miles of public land located south and west of my home, and I couldn't wait for deer season to come.

After nearly wearing out a pair of leather boots scouting, I finally settled on a stand overlooking a trail along the edge of a large beaver pond, more than two miles from where I parked my truck. Perhaps the single-biggest reason I chose to hunt the area was a rub on the trunk of a white cedar about 40 yards from my stand. The tree's trunk was nearly eight inches wide, yet the rub shredded the bark. I had never before seen a rub of such size.

On opening morning of my first northwoods deer hunt, a doe picked her way past me and took the trail along the beaver pond, and eventually disappeared. An hour later a nice 8-point buck came trotting off a far ridge, hit the doe's tracks, and turned 90 degrees to follow her ... with a reaction like that from the buck, the doe must have been in heat. Unfortunately, my stand choice wasn't quite good enough as I never got a clear view, and the buck trotted off without my firing a shot. I went home that night disappointed but determined to be back before dawn the next morning.

I was awake most of that night with the flu, but was back in my stand a half-hour before shooting light. About 8:45 that morning I heard the *crunch, crunch, crunch* of another deer trotting from the same ridge as the 8-pointer the day before, and as it materialized through the underbrush I was delighted to spot a brute of a buck with an even larger set of antlers. Fortunately, I had repositioned my stand and now had a clear view of the trail. When my crosshairs found the chest I squeezed the trigger and soon I was standing over my first northwoods buck.

The animal carried a heavy 11-point rack, and I was elated even though I now faced a 2-mile drag on dry ground. I was only three years removed from college football and still had a lineman's strength (or so I thought), and after I tagged and gutted the deer a friend and I began the death march of a drag back to the truck. About nine hours later we swung the hulk into the bed of my pick-up. I was so tired that I was falling asleep between pulls, my head resting on the buck's ribcage. At the registration station the buck weighed 202 pounds field-dressed.

The dry ground had worn the hair off the buck's left shoulder and hip, and later the taxidermist wanted to use a different cape, which I refused. I told him to make the mount look as good as possible because I didn't work that hard dragging the buck to use somebody else's cape. The mount still looks great, and the funky-looking shoulder has sparked a lot of great conversation and memories.

Since that first year I've hunted in a lot of different north-woods locations in the United States and Canada. I couldn't imagine hunting anywhere else.

The big buck I killed my first year in the northwoods was a tremendous introduction, but an incident the following year kept me solidly grounded. I had figured the buck I shot was the one that had made the big rub on the cedar tree, but a year later while scouting I was surprised to find the very same cedar had been rubbed again, only on the other side. That told me I had a lot more to learn about northwoods buck hunting — maybe I killed the buck that made the rub, but why another buck would choose the same tree made me question whether bucks were territorial. If it was a different buck that had made the rub and he was now a year older and making his mark on the same tree, I knew I would have to improve my skills to hope to take him.

Recently, I read a quote that stated "The more I learned the more I realized how little I knew." I find it very fitting to this matter of northwoods deer hunting.

I may have more than three decades of experience hunting northwoods bucks and have now written a book about the subject, but I will be the first to tell you that there are times when I feel I know nothing about it at all. It is my hope that you, like me, are a student of northwoods whitetails, and that something I've written may help you in your quest to be a better hunter. If not, I hope you enjoy some of my stories ... maybe they'll bring back fond memories of your own.

— *Steve Heiting*
May 2014

The author's regular hunting and fishing partner, Kevin Schmidt, took this 9-pointer while hunting in Ontario.

INTRODUCTION: ON THE HUNT FOR NORTHWOODS BUCKS

Scanning the woods that surround your deer stand, you spot the first few flakes of snow skate through the pine boughs. The breeze brushes your face and a flake clings to an eyelash. You blink, and the snowflake transforms into a drop that falls to your cheek. As the snowfall quickens it begins to hiss against tree branches and the dead, brown leaves on the ground. Eventually the hissing stops as the frozen burden of the gray skies turns your world white, and then ... *there!* Instantly your heart skips as a horizontal brown form oozes between the vertical trunks of trees in the distance. It stops, and your eyes strain to find the deer that has melted into the backdrop. And then you spot the black nose ... and then two black eyes encircled by white and the ears and then the antlers. With the instinct borne of many seasons in the deer woods, you ease the safety off and shoulder your rifle.

Another day, another season. The snow is a deep blue and squeaks as you hustle for the warmth of camp. It's the end of the day and your cheeks are raw while a drop quivers from the end of your nose. The chill that came when you sucked frigid air into your lungs when you got up to leave your stand is still with you as a shiver crawls up your spine. It's been a good day — even though you didn't see a deer — because gunfire nearby has told you somebody in camp got a buck. As you round a bend in the trail, a gaslight dances yellow in the snow in front of your deer camp's window, and laughter roars from inside. Barely lit by the flickering edges of the glow, a dark form hangs from a horizontal pole behind the camp. Rather than heading toward the shack's door and the warmth it contains, you make a slight detour to count antler points.

Another day, another season. Black patches of earth have been ripped open through the leaves on the trail, and dirt spray points back toward the swamp, right where you suspected the big boy lives. A deeply-printed track leads toward the ridge, where a new scar on the trunk of a white cedar glows in what passes for daylight in November. Opening Day is tomorrow and one final check of your stand — you couldn't help yourself — has revealed more than you really needed to find. After all, you had intended to get a good night's sleep.

Another day, in April. The snow that fell in November has finally seeped into the ground and trickled into the swamps. Since darkness overtook the final day of the hunt last fall, you've sought a better stand. You've studied your topographical map and satellite photos and think ... no, hope, that the funnel you've spotted and can't believe you missed previously will be *the one*. It's time to make tracks. Compass, map and GPS in hand, you head out, and as you follow the funnel you begin to find rubs ... lots of rubs, and a couple scrapes for good measure. And there, in the soft earth of spring, you spot it — the large hoof print with the right toe slightly crossed over the left. *He* made it! The buck that eluded you last fall — except for that early November morning when an unseen twig deflected your arrow harmlessly over his back — has survived the winter and will be there to challenge you again this year.

If all of the above appeals to you, then you are a northwoods buck hunter.

Those who hunt the northwoods for white-tailed deer know theirs is not so much a place to hunt as it is a calling. The northwoods is a place where adventure — not another hunter — waits around the bend in the trail, where a deer hunt is a chess match that yields more frustration than venison, and where success is often measured only by the warmth in your soul when you know you've given your all. It's a place where a hunter can usually walk as far as his legs will take him, where the only boundaries he will often see are those he places upon himself.

The northwoods is often big woods, where public lands are

The author's friend, Paul Bietka, smiles over his 16-pointer. Bucks like this draw hunters to the northwoods.

open to all and extend for miles, not acres. The true northwoods hunter must be willing to go *to* the deer and hunt for days, either from a stand or afoot, until the buck he wants appears in the crosshairs of his scope or the peepsight of his bow. And if it doesn't happen today, he'll get up before dawn tomorrow and do it again, and again, and again, and maybe every morning until there are no more days left in the season.

THE NORTHWOODS BUCK

Deer populations of the northwoods are often miniscule when compared to other areas. I recall listening to a Wisconsin wildlife biologist at a meeting where he called deer numbers of 10 or fewer per square mile "practically unhuntable," yet this is a common population estimate in many of the places I have hunted. Bucks in the northwoods must endure frigid overnight temperatures and chest-deep snow in winter, the uncertainty of spring when winter lingers and gnaws at their rut- and winter-stressed bodies, and the constant threat of predators. Is the buck even conscious of its own precarious mortality when a full moon rises in the clear skies of a brutally-cold January night? I doubt it, but it readily endures such hardships because to the buck it's nothing more than everyday life.

When fall comes and his antlers harden, the northwoods buck runs the gauntlet of hunters. The basic tenet of Quality Deer Management, as practiced in more agricultural areas, is to shoot abundant does and let the bucks go so they can grow. This is but a pipe dream on public lands of the north, especially in areas where antlerless tags are few and far between because of low deer populations. I can't fault the hunter who is hungry for venison and shoots a yearling buck on Opening Day because he doesn't have a doe tag in his pocket. That small buck he takes home may be his only chance to put a deer in the freezer that season. I know, because I've been there myself.

If you hunt northwoods bucks, you know the odds are already stacked against you. If there are 10 deer per square mile, fewer than half of them will be antlered bucks. There's a lot of acreage between them. You may have to search through several square miles of timber to find a single buck that is 3½ years old or more, and then when his nomadic nature kicks in during fall he'll make things even tougher for you.

When biologists give an estimate of 10 or 20 or whatever deer per square mile, the deer aren't spread evenly throughout the landscape. For the most part they live in pockets, where bedding cover, food and water are sufficient for their needs. Predators and logging — as well as factors not entirely understood — can affect these pockets.

Logging is very important to wilderness whitetails because opening up the forest floor to sunlight will allow all kinds of deer food to sprout. Stands of short popple (trembling aspen) and willow are key found sources. Yet I have set up hunting stands in such areas that looked terrific on the surface, and in many cases the set-ups were almost identical to others that were productive elsewhere, and when it came time to hunt them they were complete busts. That's the way it goes when you have few deer living in giant timbered areas. However, if you find a couple areas with doe groups living in them, big bucks will find the does at the time of the rut.

The northwoods buck is a homebody for much of the summer and early fall, but that will change. When he is living in a bachelor group and feeding on a warm summer's evening in an opening caused by logging, he gives one the idea that he will be easily-patternable and a sure thing. I've fallen hard for this idea before and will likely do so again. Once the big buck sheds the velvet from his antlers in early September he will become less tolerant of his buddies and, often, virtually disappear. Sure, the spikes and forkhorns of the bachelor group remain, but the big one — whose antlers you had hoped to hang on your wall — will be gone. When a buck does this you'll be very fortunate to find him again, even as the laziness of October's sunny afternoons gives way to the frenzy of the November rut.

Once the rut comes, a big buck may show up just out of your bow range in a forest opening today, and appear tomorrow in a photo taken by your buddy's trail camera 10 miles away. He's on the move, looking for does, and if his home range is huge the distance he will travel can be mind-boggling. If you're lucky to have a resident doe come into heat near one of your trail cameras, the number of big bucks that will show up in photos can be amazing. A day or so later after the doe has been bred, the bucks will be gone.

This is why hunting northwoods bucks can be such a physical and mental challenge. A hunter needs to be there and be there, and be there some more, until the buck he *thinks* he's hunting, or another one just like him, shows up in front of his stand. And, he may be hunting for an animal that doesn't even exist anymore because it made the mistake of walking too closely to another hunter perched in a tree miles away, or it chased a doe onto a road where it met a pick-up truck head-on and lost.

For all these reasons, a northwoods buck that lives to the age of 3½ years or more is a special animal. He has seen it all, from packs of wolves on his trail to tree-splitting cold, to the drives and trail cameras and bait piles of man. His antlers usually will not measure up to those of his comparably-aged cousins in farm country, but he is a trophy nonetheless. Often those same antlers will appear at first glance to be smaller than they really are, because northwoods bucks tend to grow outsize bodies. A really big buck will weigh 200 pounds or more field-dressed.

This is the kind of buck I consider my goal every time I step into the woods. I would like to set my goal even higher and

hope for even older bucks, but given the odds stacked against north-woods deer I have to be realistic.

When all your scouting efforts and boot leather and pre-season preparation and time in the woods come together and a big buck steps in front of your sights, and you make the shot, the feeling is indescribable. Holding his antlers in your hands is the ultimate triumph because on that day, somehow in some way, you were something the buck couldn't over-come.

Northwoods bucks' antlers often have character. Note the extra beam on the left antler of Ryan Adams' buck.

The northwoods buck is a survivor whose very existence depends on his ability to detect danger, or his innate sixth sense that in some way tells him when it is not wise to move forward. If matching wits with an animal like this appeals to you, then you are a northwoods buck hunter.

HUNTING THE NORTHWOODS

I have come full circle in the way I hunt northwoods deer. I started as a stand-hunter, then joined and eventually bought membership in a deer camp where still-hunting — what we call

23

"poke and mosey" — is tradition. However, I eventually reverted to stand-hunting when I realized my still-hunting efforts were not producing the kind of bucks I wanted. I am not saying the guys in camp are wrong; rather, their way of hunting on their own doesn't work as well for me. I am not sure why — perhaps my feet are too big. Hunting at the camp is an annual tradition, but while everyone else pokes and moseys the first few days, I will be seated in a tree stand.

I admit my way is not exactly the romantic notion of a single hunter tracking his quarry through the northwoods, but in this day and age it is often the only realistic option. In my home state of Wisconsin, the north is hunted hard. Not by the numbers of hunters that you'll find in the southern and central parts of the state, but if you take a track you will eventually run into another hunter, and likely more. You could also easily drive the buck you hope to shoot to another hunter. Another factor is that parcels of public land are often intertwined with private holdings, and when the buck you're chasing crosses the property

A trail camera photo of a huge-bodied northwoods buck. With rolls on his neck, he is likely over 300 pounds live weight.

line, you have no option but to turn back. Still-hunters can be successful, but the size of the bucks they kill is limited to what is currently present where they hunt. Rather than picking out a track by size and following it, their hope of a big buck is based on the chance that one is in the woods they hunt that day. I know this isn't the situation in other states and provinces, but stand-hunting pays off for me in those locales, too, so I've decided to try to get really good at it.

It was on a March day when I realized that if I really wanted to change my big buck fortunes I needed to take control of the factors that I could. What a good friend says about musky fishing applies to lots of other things, including deer hunting: "If you always do what you've always done, you will always get what you've always got."

I decided that day to make a handful of changes in the way I hunt deer. The changes were simple but dramatic, relatively inexpensive, and have paid off with annual close-range encounters with bucks of 3½ years of age or better. The best part about the changes is they could be made by anyone.

Perhaps most important, I realized that I had been my own worst enemy when hunting deer. Following are the changes that I've made:

1.) With the exception of evening bow-hunts after work, or when my deer camp decides it's a "drive day," I hunt from a stand the entire day without leaving.

During the time when I had bought into the romance of still-hunting, I saw some country, put a lot of miles on my boots, and killed only one big buck and several small ones. And tracking? Only once have I taken an unwounded buck's track and killed it. Most of the big bucks I saw while still-hunting had spotted me first and were rapidly putting acreage between us by the time I saw them. Big bucks don't get that way by letting just anyone blunder into them.

2.) I gave myself more opportunity to succeed. Because the fall months are considered "trophy time" for muskies, for years I chased big fish and my deer hunting consisted only of Wisconsin's 9-day gun-hunt. But then I bought a muzzleloader and added as many as 10 more days to my season. One fall I walked into an archery shop and asked the proprietor to sell me a bow, and this simple step added hundreds of mornings and evenings in a deer stand — talk about a bargain! You can be the most-skilled hunter to have ever walked the woods, but if you don't give yourself opportunity you won't kill many big bucks. Since deer are relatively scarce in the northwoods and big bucks are even more rare, time is your ally.

Like almost anyone else, my time in the woods is limited by work constraints, but I am fortunate in that thousands of acres of state-owned property open to public hunting are located within 15 minutes of my office, and I spend considerable time bow-hunting there after work. Now, I have killed more big bucks with my rifle and muzzleloader than my bow, but that is to be expected given the challenges bow-hunting presents. (Anybody who thinks bow-hunters have it easy because of longer seasons should try it first. I, too, thought it would be much easier than it is.) But the bucks I have shot with a bow never would have been tagged had I not walked into the archery shop. Practically every evening in the woods on a deer stand is an education, so that alone has made me a better hunter.

3.) I've added an annual out-of-state deer hunt to my repertoire. Whether you book an outfitter or go the do-it-yourself route depends on your pocketbook, your desires and the laws where you travel, but seeing different deer woods, possibly learning new ways to hunt, and spending more time in a stand are beneficial. And, let's face it, other locales may harbor bigger deer than your customary deer woods.

4.) I changed my viewpoint of what I consider a deer worth

shooting. As stated earlier, I have no problem with the guy who wants to eat a deer and takes a small buck, but it almost goes without saying that if you shoot the first buck you see you won't kill many big ones — there just aren't that many of them! However, if you bow-hunt, gun-hunt, muzzleloader-hunt, and throw in an out-of-state hunt when you can, chances are that somewhere along the line you'll shoot a good one. This makes it more palatable to let lesser bucks walk.

5.) Finally, I have embraced modern technology, at least in the form of scent-containing clothing and trail cameras. I often yearn for the old ways, but modern technology can really help. I will explain more in the chapter, "The Equipment Equation."

So, as you read on, you'll find that I primarily focus on stand-hunting because this is what has produced my biggest northwoods bucks. But I have killed lots of bucks and does while still-hunting, tracking and driving, and have driven lots of deer to hunters posted on stands during drives, so there will be extensive discussion of these tactics.

Whether you take a stand or a track, succeeding in the northwoods involves the commitment of being there, and being there, and being there some more until the buck you want shows itself. If this appeals to you, then you are a northwoods buck hunter.

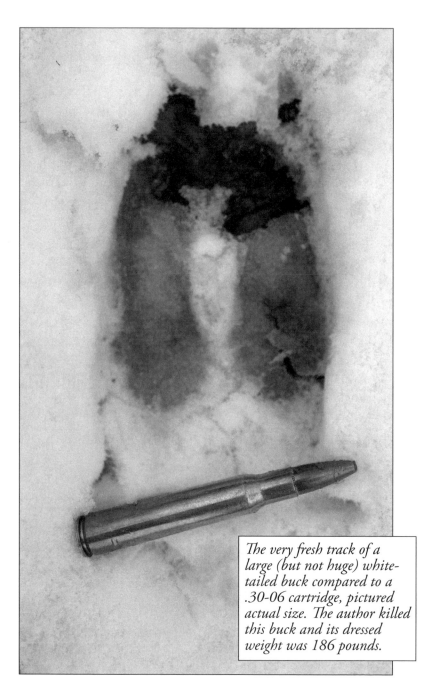

The very fresh track of a large (but not huge) white-tailed buck compared to a .30-06 cartridge, pictured actual size. The author killed this buck and its dressed weight was 186 pounds.

WHAT THE BUCKS TELL US

Iwill never forget the first set of truly big buck tracks that I had ever seen. Pressed deep into the mud, with dewclaws evident and toes pointed slightly outward, it appeared as if the devil himself had walked the Earth the night before. I tried to match its gait and my stride proved uncomfortable. Yet, here was a giant buck's unmistakable track left in a logging road.

As they go about their daily lives, bucks leave a trail of clues for the observant hunter. One does not need to be a detective to kill a big buck, but the more you know about the animal you are hunting the greater your chances of taking him. And, taking note of how bucks are influenced by the environment will make you a better hunter. Weather — and even the moon — impact their daily lives.

THE TRAIL BUCKS LEAVE

Every step a buck takes leaves a track, likely thousands every day. Outside of seeing the buck itself, finding a big track or catching him in a photo taken by a trail camera are the only sure ways to know that a large buck has visited the area. A rub on a fairly-wide tree is also a good indicator. Large scrapes are often considered a sign of a big buck, but since several bucks may work the same scrape its reliability in estimating the bucks' sizes is less than accurate.

A big buck's track will be wide; lay a large centerfire rifle shell crossways on the track and the width will be very close to the length of the cartridge. Dewclaws may be evident in mud, snow or sand, but not on leaves or in pine needles. A trail of large, black holes punched through brown pine needles is a good indicator of a large buck. The more heavy and broad-chested the buck, the greater the spread between the tracks of his right and left hooves. Usually, his toes will point slightly outward. Though a big buck probably is not doing so purposely, his track will appear as if he walks with a swagger. While walking in a couple inches of snow, a large buck will often drag his toes, but the deeper the snow gets the greater the likelihood that any deer will drags its toes, so this isn't always a good indicator of size.

A big buck is an old buck, and age increases the possibility of abnormalities in his hooves. These could be chips, overlapping toes, a toe longer than another, or some kind of injury. You can recognize an individual buck by these abnormalities when they press into soft soil or snow. In the days before trail cameras, this was often the only way to know that a particular buck had survived from one year to the next, or was in the area. Deer tracks that are symmetrical and form perfect "split hearts" are usually made by does and small bucks, animals that are smaller and typically younger.

Another indicator the track you are checking has been made by a large buck is the distance between trees through which he walked. A broad-chested buck with a large set of antlers is not about to squeeze through narrow gaps in the forest growth. He may choose to walk where trees are wider-spaced, and his tracks will often swing wide to bypass a tight opening. For this reason, hunting near an edge where older trees meet a clearcut can be effective. The buck can easily travel in the old growth yet have abundant food sources a step or two away. Whitetails are always creatures of the edge, and this may be one of the reasons why.

Let the trees the buck walks between be a gauge of the width of his antlers. A buck that picks routes where trees grow closely together probably does not have a big rack.

The width of their chest and antlers may also explain why larger bucks seem to like overhead cover, in the form of pines, cedars, balsam fir or spruce. In walking through taller growth, the cover to his sides may not provide sufficient comfort, so he seeks it from above. Unless he is chasing a doe, a big buck will rarely walk far into the new growth of a clearcut during the day. The older the buck the more prone he is to favor moving in low-light or at night, and perhaps dense conifer cover tricks him into feeling secure. Regardless, the more I hunt these animals the more time I spend on the edge of such "dark timber."

Deer tracks age with time. This may not be so important for the stand-hunter, for as long as there are tracks of reasonable age where he hunts he maintains a good chance of seeing a buck. But aging tracks is necessary to the business of the still-hunter or tracker, so he must learn to master the art.

The edges of a fresh track are sharp, regardless if they are in soft soil or snow. Wind, rain, snow or the sun will erode, melt or blunt these edges; just how hard the wind is blowing or the rain or snow is falling, or how directly the sun is hitting the trail, will determine the aging of the track. A good way of aging a track is to look at one's own track and notice how quickly its edges soften.

A track that has water or unfrozen soil in it on a below-freezing day is a fresh one. However, ice in a track may not be reason to consider it old because a track will freeze fairly rapidly on a cold day. Thin ice in the track may indicate the buck is only an hour or so ahead. Bend down and stick your fingers into the track to gauge the thickness of the ice. If a track is still filling up with water the buck is likely within range and it's time to search him out before you take your next step.

Bucks that are looking for does may cover a lot of ground with long strides. If his tracks meet up with a second, smaller deer, it is likely he has found his doe and the tracks may show them running as he prods her to mate. If the buck leaves lots of meandering tracks in a small area he is likely feeding and will bed soon. When hunting in snow you will often see pieces of the browse lying among his tracks, something you will have to watch for closely when hunting over brown leaves. If the tracks are fresh and you think the buck was feeding, he is likely very close and your movements must be deathly slow.

OTHER BUCK SIGN

Bucks leave two calling cards as they prepare for the rut — rubs on trees, and scrapes on the ground. The purpose of each is a matter of debate. It is generally accepted that bucks make scrapes before and during the rut to announce their presence to does. Rubs are made to remove velvet from antlers, to work off aggression when does are not yet ready to breed, to build up neck muscles for the rut, and to mark a buck's territory visually and with scent. Lots of rubs in an area may indicate you've found a buck's bedroom, but you definitely have found a route he likes to walk.

Bucks seem to really like what the author calls "dark timber," where conifer growth may give the buck a feeling of security. They seem more prone to move during the day in such places.

Scrapes are pawings in the earth where a buck uses its hooves to clear the soil of leaves, grass and other debris, and then urinates on the bare earth. Often the buck will leave a large hoof print in the scrape; whether this is intentional or not is open to discussion. I tend to think a buck's hoofprint in the middle of a scrape is mere coincidence, but it is a good sign if the hoof print is large because you know a big buck has used the scrape. Almost always the scrape will have an overhanging branch, which the buck will lick, and rub with his forehead and the glands around his eyes to deposit scent. Scrapes will usually be made on flat terrain, but a logging road on a slight incline may be littered with them.

This large scrape lies before a rubbed tag alder. Note how the alder has tried to heal its scar from several years of rubbing.

Do not get caught up in the excitement of the first scrapes of fall. Younger bucks seem to come into rut before older bucks and tend to open a lot of these scrapes. In fact, I have watched yearling bucks make scrapes as early as late September. Scrapes that are part of the rutting season will follow. These will almost always will have an overhanging branch and many will be alongside a rub.

Scrape size has little to do with the size of the buck. Rather, scrapes in obvious areas tend to be worked by several bucks and

For years bucks have rubbed on this particular tree on a swamp edge. Note how the bark has tried to grow back around to close off the scarred area.

this may be the reason why some scrapes are larger than others.

Rublines often will not be on the main deer path but on an obscure trail off to the side. The main trail is often the one used by does, fawns and young bucks, but the larger bucks' trails will be a lot less obvious. Often, this is simply because fewer deer will use this trail. Always remember that rubs will usually be on the side of the tree opposite the direction the buck is headed — if the buck is headed north, his rubs will be on the south side of the tree. Along with that, the dirt from scrapes will often be pawed in the opposite direction — a north-heading buck's pawing will be on the south side of the scrape. When you find dirt thrown in at least two different directions from the scrape, you know bucks have visited the scrape from different directions. If you find a trail with numerous rubs and scrapes on a trail leading away from an area that is known to be used by deer for bedding, this spot would be a good choice for an afternoon hunt. Conversely, if you found the rubs and scrapes heading toward a bedding area, this would be a good place for an early morning hunt.

Often, generations of bucks will rub on the same tree. Marking on this particular tree apparently means something in the deer world; perhaps it's where buck territories overlap. The bark may try to grow back around to close off the scar, yet the deer continue to rub there. Considering this, hunting from a stand near such a rub or rubs is a good idea.

I may be criticized for saying this, but as much as I've read about rublines I still cannot figure out how to determine that the rubs made in one location were made by the same buck a mile away, and all I need to do is connect the dots to find a good stand to kill this buck. I have learned to identify the differences in deer hoofprints to track individual animals, but I question hunters who state that a particular buck made a certain rub

There are a number of reasons why bucks make rubs. Often they are made to mark a buck's territory. This rub was found along a trail leading to a large bedding area.

because a groove in the rubbed tree may match a sticker point on his antler burr. Now, I do not doubt that some can do this, but it is one skill that to date has escaped me.

There was one season at my deer camp when several of us found rubs that were in the oddest of locations. In many cases, a buck had rubbed a sapling that was set back and within a tangle of other saplings, or slightly downhill from where the buck was standing while making the rub — the rub was on the uphill side.

Some were made in the middle of a tree, rather than near the bottom of the trunk. Apparently this buck liked having some kind of difficulty in making his rubs. Oddities like this are probably particular to one buck, but rarely are such examples found this often.

Big bucks also leave large beds. Usually, they will be by themselves unless they are bedded with a doe during the rut. Size alone should give away a buck bed, but if there is any question, a buck's bed in snow will often be stained near its middle. This is from urine from the penis or may be from the hocks or metatarsal glads, upon which a buck will urinate during the rut.

A large buck will also have an odor which can be quite noticeable on damp days, or where the air is trapped by thick brush, even when there is snow on the ground. Bucks that have been rutting hard will smell the strongest. I have smelled this odor hanging in the air many times, usually after I have just pushed out a buck during a drive. Does will also have an odor, but a buck will often be rank.

WHITETAILS & WEATHER

Deer hunters have no control over the weather, yet the weather may control our success for the day. All a hunter can do is make the best of the conditions at hand.

If there is a guarantee when it comes to the various weather conditions, it is that northwoods bucks do not like warm weather. Once the daytime temperature reaches about 40 degrees Fahrenheit, the higher it goes the lower the chance of seeing deer during the day. If the temperature tops 50, there is almost no chance of seeing a buck from a stand (except in early bow season). It may seem that the deer have disappeared from the woods, except that hunters driving home after dark may see several. The evening air is cool and the deer are on the move.

The way I see it, hunters may think the air temperature is

warm, yet the deer are the ones wearing fur coats. They are forced to live in the conditions and most often choose to lay low until things cool down. If there are any places where a buck may be on his feet during the day, it's in a river bottom, out of the sun along a north-facing slope, or in a swamp, but the chances remain slim.

When the longterm weather forecast calls for an extended period of warm weather during hunting season, a deer hunter may have to lower his standards if he hopes to fill his tag and an opportunity at a smaller buck presents itself. One season my camp woke to 20-degree air temperatures on Opening Day, though the predicted high for the day was in the mid 50s and the longterm forecast called for highs from 50 to 60 each day. The camp members shot two bucks and missed a third on the opener, yet did not see another buck the remainder of the season in spite of making drives almost every day. Sure, we collectively saw a couple does each day, but no bucks. I decided to shoot a 5-pointer standing 20 yards away just two hours after legal shooting light on the opener, figuring that it would be my only chance at venison that season. It was.

Warm weather may also delay the start of the rut. Photoperiodism and the moon are usually the key triggers to the rut, but when air temperatures are warm the rut may be delayed, or rutting activity may only occur at night.

Cold weather, on the other hand, seems to kick-start the rut. And, the colder it is during the rest of the fall, the more likely it seems that bucks are willing to move during the day. Hunters plagued by warm weather pray for it to change, and once cold air arrives hunting usually becomes pretty good. Canadian outfitters note a marked difference in the success of their hunters once cold conditions arrive.

A rapid change from warm weather to cold is usually brought about by dramatic storms, often with high winds and heavy rain or snow. If there is one thing that will get lounging bucks on the move, it is the coming of a major weather front. Once, while on an out-of-state hunt, three of the four stands watched by our trail cameras had 3½-year-old or better bucks visit them in daylight the morning before a huge storm hit that night, and I shot a 10-pointer from the one stand where we had not placed a camera. All told, four of our five stands had quality bucks in front of them the morning preceding the storm!

The deer will limit their movements for the duration of the storm, but once it passes they will be up on their feet. The first "normal" day following a storm that lasts several days can be terrific.

High winds put bucks on alert because they cannot see well as branches and foliage are constantly moving, and the wind blocks their hearing and quickly whisks away scent. If branches or trees are breaking and falling, such conditions can be hazardous for hunters. However, if the conditions are windy yet not dangerous, this is the day a hunter can sneak closely to a bedded buck. A stand-hunter will probably struggle to see deer, but a tracker or still-hunter who spends his day in a bedding area may kill a giant.

Rain is a condition that I would prefer to not hunt. Unless I am under the cover of a nylon ground blind, a steady rain will eventually soak through my clothing and I will have to clean my rifle. When I wore eyeglasses, I hated having to wipe them as they became streaked and spotted. A blood trail can be very difficult to follow if rain washes most of it away. Yet rain can be a productive condition for the deer hunter as it washes his scent from the air, the ground and any brush he may have contacted on the way to his stand, and, like snow, quiets the woods. A drizzly day seems to put the deer at ease and they will often be on the move. For these reasons I enjoy hunting in a drizzle.

Snow that falls in late October or early November may melt

the next day as the weather changes. As the snow melts and drips from trees, the conditions are very similar to a drizzly day. Deer will usually be at ease and on the move.

THOUGHTS ON HUNTING IN SNOW

There are many ways by which snow can help the deer hunter. It brightens and often eliminates the dull grays and browns of the fall woods and helps us see farther and clearer. Snow makes deer easier to see because they stand out in contrast. If a deer is not killed by a hunter's first shot, snow makes the animal's tracks and blood trail easier to follow. And, snow can silence a hunter's movements through the deer woods.

The deer themselves seem to enjoy the first snow of the season. The day after the front passes, the woods are filled with deer tracks. It is as if the woods are so different that the deer's curiosity causes them to check out their new surroundings. Where I live in northern Wisconsin, the first measurable snow of the year always seems to fall during the last week of October or the first week of November, and the days that follow often yield some of the most memorable bow-hunts of the entire season. I feel energized when I enter the forest because I strongly believe that I will see deer on such days and, often, I am right.

Snow also means cold. On the coldest days of late fall, which are usually sunny at the same time, a great place to hunt is a south-facing slope. The sun will feel good to you regardless if you take a stand or still-hunt, and deer will enjoy it, too.

As much as I enjoy hunting in snow, you can count me as one who would almost prefer to not see it. Snow can be beneficial, but it can also bring a lot of frustration.

My first reason for not wanting to see snow is that like anything else, I leave tracks. If other hunters did not have the propensity to follow another's tracks, I would not have a problem with this. However, one season I had two large 8-point bucks spotted in a section of state-owned land where a long ridge led into a swamp. I hunted this ridge a lot during the rut in the belief that it was only a matter of time before one of the bucks offered me a shot, so my truck was often parked on the side of the road near this ridge. One day it snowed, and the next day I enjoyed one of those amazing outings in which everything almost comes together yet does not. I drew three times that afternoon at one of the 8-pointers and a different buck that I had not previously seen, yet never fired a shot because a clear opportunity at either animal never presented itself.

Only days remained before the gun-deer hunting season, which I knew would change the deer's patterns considerably. I could not wait to hunt the next day because I knew time was running out. The next afternoon, while walking into the same stand, I found another set of boot tracks in my tracks from the day before. When I reached the tree where I hung my climbing stand, I discovered that someone else had set up a bait in the exact location I had been hunting! Now, this occurred on state-owned land and the other hunter had the same right as I to hunt there, but never before had I seen any sign of others in the area until I left tracks in the snow. The fact the other hunter set up in the same location could not be coincidental.

Being somewhat bullheaded, I continued to hunt the stand and kept an eye out for the other hunter. He continued to bait the stand but never showed while I was there. With this added intrusion, the bucks never showed themselves to me again. As it turned out, the other hunter was setting up his bait for the approaching gun-hunting season and wound up shooting an antlerless deer from the stand.

Maybe I'm wrong to blame snow for the actions of another hunter, but snow itself is seldom prime for hunting. If snow would fall on a cold day and the air temperatures would remain well below freezing, the snow may be preserved and all the benefits it can provide may be realized for a long time. But too often snow falls on ground that has not yet frozen, which almost immediately creates a slight crust between the snow and leaves. Wet snow may cling to everything, drastically obscuring visibility. As every hunter knows, such snow will cling until one tries to sneak under a laden branch — then it drops down the back of the hunter's neck. If the snow freezes to the tree branches, it could be days before the sun or wind knock it from the tree trunks and branches.

The last decade or so, snow days seem to be followed by a warm front which can cause the snow to crust over, making for noisy walking for both hunters and deer. Snow that melts completely may soak into the dead leaves, and when temperatures drop those same leaves will crunch beneath your feet like corn flakes the next morning. Every deer in the woods will know you are there.

Though deer have to go about their lives in any condition, including crunchy snow, if they know they are being hunted they will become most difficult to kill. I can think of only a couple of bucks that I have taken in extremely crunchy conditions, and all of them were killed from a stand on the first or second day of the hunt. One year I was positioned on a saddle overlooking a ravine, and when a loud, steady crunching developed on the flat across the ravine I was dismayed as I believed it to be another hunter coming my way. I was shocked when the noisemaker turned out to be a handsome 8-pointer, which I shot as it crossed the ravine in front of me.

Snow has a lot of benefits for the deer hunter. If I know that it will stay favorable and not turn crunchy, or I can be assured that no one will use it to steal my hard-scouted hunting spots, I will take it. Otherwise, count me as one who would just as soon not see it.

THE RUTTING (AND FEEDING) MOON

If you have been a deer hunter for any length of time, you surely must have heard of the "rutting moon." This is considered to be the second full moon following the autumnal equinox (the first day of fall) and is thought by some to be what takes the rut into full swing.

I have tried to predict hunts according to the rutting moon and then been thwarted in my plans by warm weather, which delayed the rut or turned it into a nighttime activity. Still, there have been times when this moon period has yielded fantastic hunting.

Every year there seems to be a day or two when big bucks are on the move and everybody sees them and many kill them. It was November 6 one year when I called a friend, John Stellflue, with my cellphone to tell him about the 8-point buck that lay at my feet, which I had arrowed a mere 30 minutes before. "You're not going to believe it, but I'm standing over an 11-pointer right now!" John shouted into his telephone. Later, as we talked with others, we found November 6 was productive seemingly every-where. Even the proprietor of my local bow shop hesitated when I told him I got my buck on November 6. "There were a lot of big bucks that died that day," he told me. The moon set that day at 2:59 p.m. and John and I both arrowed our bucks minutes after 3.

The moon can make deer hunting predictable, but not always for reasons of the rut. Conventional wisdom is that a bright moon at night will turn deer nocturnal. However, from my ob-servations, as well as those of others, deer do not like a bright moon at night. You can judge this for yourself — the next time you are driving home at night under a bright full moon, how many deer will you see? There will always be the odd deer or two, but for the most part deer activity will cease and you will not have to concern yourself much with striking a deer with your car.

The author (left) arrowed this 8-point buck on the day following the first snowfall of the year. It was taken at almost precisely the moment his friend, John Stellflue (right), who was hunting 30 miles away, killed an 11-pointer.

A friend once explained to me how he can predict good evenings for bow-hunting: "Do you ever wonder why there are some days when the fields and roadsides are full of deer in the afternoon?" he asked. "They're feeding ahead of moonrise. The moon will be up most of the night and for some reason they don't like it."

My buddy works in a large manufacturing plant with some 500 employees, many of whom bow-hunt. A supervisor would make the rounds of known bow-hunters and ask them how they did the previous evening. On the evenings when the moon was to rise or set just before nightfall, the evening hunting was superb.

When the moon would rise after the close of legal hunting hours, the hunting was average to below average. With time, this supervisor could predict the prime afternoons and evenings for bowhunting and would schedule his own vacation time months in advance.

Apparently, deer do not want to be up and about at night when the moon is in the sky. The times just before the moon is to rise, and the times just after it sets, are prime to be in the woods, especially if they coincide with daybreak or nightfall. Still, a moon rising or setting at any time of the day or night can produce sudden deer action. Though the moon's influence seems more pronounced during full or new moon periods, any moonrise or set could bring deer activity. Many of those who fish for muskies have made the same correlation.

Now, I will hunt when I can and the conditions are right for my stands, regardless of the moon. You never know what a rut-crazed buck will do. But since I have begun paying attention to the moon I have noticed that the times predicted by my friend and his supervisor are often better than average. When I killed my best buck ever on the day of the full moon, during a brief, magic window between moonrise and sunset, I was not surprised. This was also during a "Minor Period" predicted by John Alden Knight's Solunar Tables, on a day that was ranked high for fish and game activity.

Remember, local weather will always trump the moon. But if one pays attention to the moon and the effect it can have on white-tailed deer, it can be an eye-opening experience.

The scrape and well-used trail are obvious. What you do not see is that this trail funnels between a beaver pond and a high ridge. This is one to hunt!

FINDING THE PERFECT DEER STAND

L et's get this right out in the open — I have yet to find the perfect deer stand. I have some good ones, including one from which I killed 11- and 15-point bucks in consecutive years, but it is not perfect. To me, a perfect deer stand is in an area of high deer activity that can be hunted almost without regard to the wind thanks to its vantage point. My stand would also be of sufficient distance from where I would expect to see deer, so I will not alert them with slight movement, but not so far as to make shooting a difficult proposition. This perfect stand would have easy access so my entry to the woods will not spook any deer from the area.

In over three decades of hunting the northwoods I have not found such a stand. But I keep trying.

SCOUTING

I begin looking for a deer stand by studying road maps and topographical maps for large areas of unbroken timber because places that are difficult to access will contain fewer hunters. All of my best stands for rifle hunting have been located at least a half-mile from the nearest road accessible to a 4-wheel-drive truck, and one stand I have used is 2.9 miles from where I park my truck. Every one of my biggest bucks that had a dressed weight of 200 pounds or more were shot from a stand at least a mile from my truck. If there are fewer hunters, the chance of finding a buck that has survived a couple of seasons to grow a respectable rack is much higher. It is also more likely that this big buck will be undisturbed and following his normal routine.

In this day of increasing rural development, it is common to find places where public land borders on private holdings, and in some cases entire subdivisions — even in the northwoods. Deer numbers on such public land tend to be higher than places where there are no homes because people like to feed deer to watch them in their backyard, and plants and shrubbery around the homes tend to be high on the deer's favored food list. Such public land spots can be good for a big buck early in the bow season before buck bachelor groups break up, and then again during the rut when bucks are cruising for does. If the recreational feeding continues into December, bigger bucks that are worn down from the rut sometimes move into these areas for the easy food. For the most part, though, if you want a big buck you will have to go to where he lives.

I conduct most of my deer scouting in the springtime between the times of snowmelt and green-up, because the woods in late March and early April look a lot like they did the previous fall. Usually, deer sign from the previous autumn remains evident as trails, droppings, rubs and scrapes are still highly visible. Finding a shed can tip you off to a big buck you didn't know lived in the vicinity. Most importantly, however, any deer disturbed by my scouting in spring will have long since forgotten our encounter when it is time to begin hunting.

Still, like anybody else, I am going to check things out before I hunt because logging, the presence of other hunters, and the year's natural food will have a tremendous effect on a stand's potential. One season that comes to mind produced an acorn crop greater than I had ever seen. Practically every oak in the woods produced massive amounts of acorns, and deer that lived in areas

Deer eat almost anything, but in years of bumper acorn crops you must consider hunting near oaks. In this photo, deer have been pawing through snow for acorns.

without oaks seemingly disappeared as they relocated to places with the mast-bearing tree. I killed two bucks that fall, one with a rifle in my home state and one on an out-of-state hunt, but had I hunted the stands I had chosen the previous spring I would have been blanked. As it was, I never did figure the situation out during bow-hunting season and ended without once loosing an arrow.

I follow four criteria for choosing my deer hunting stand — deer activity, or potential for deer activity; prevailing wind; cover for my stand; and ease of access. For many, scouting for white-tails involves looking for areas with lots of recent tracks, droppings, pawed leaves and other sign, and every hunter's pulse is quickened by fresh buck rubs and scrapes. I look for these, too, but only to confirm that deer are using an area I have already scouted.

It is easy to be intimidated by big woods, but in this day of GPS and satellite imagery it needn't be that way. Understand first and foremost that you cannot hunt it all. And, no matter how much boot leather you leave behind, it will take years to learn all the nuances of your hunting area. So, I start by looking at the big picture and then narrow my focus.

After I choose an area of big timber (as discussed earlier), I drive around as much of the perimeter of the potential hunting area in the hope of getting an idea of forest type — recent clearcuts mean more food for deer but also allow for greater hunter access, while unbroken, tall timber can mean fewer hunters but will likely contain deer populations too low to bother with. I hope to find mixed growth.

If the road maps and drive-by are favorable, I next consult topographical maps and satellite photos for landforms, like swamps, waterbodies, ridges, saddles, hogsbacks, streams, timber types, and even beaver ponds. It helps sometimes to use a yellow felt marker to highlight these areas on the map. Satellite imagery such as that provided by Google Earth can show what the spots really have to offer — is the swamp on the topo map nothing but a sedge bog, or is it a nice, thick tangle of cedars? You will have a good idea before you even step into the woods, saving lots of time and boot leather. Landforms are hugely important because they influence or funnel the daily movement of northwoods deer, whether they realize it or not.

My biggest Wisconsin buck was shot as it skirted a beaver pond following a doe. The rut was in full swing and I suspect the doe was in heat, but she followed the edge of the beaver pond near the hogsback where I was sitting and the buck took the same route until he stepped into range.

He could have slogged through the beaver pond had he wanted to take the most direct route to the doe, but walking around the edge was easier. Another year, an 8-pointer that I shot while I was posted on a drive could have run through the ravine and up the other side to safety, but quartering through the ravine

Beaver ponds can dramatically alter the landscape, and definitely funnel the movements of deer.

and crossing at a low saddle was easier — at least until my rifle barked. These are two quick examples of how deer follow landforms. Like humans, they are going to take the easiest route possible. Think of landforms as barriers that force deer to change their route either for ease of travel or for cover.

It is always good to sit on the edge of a big swamp because deer will use it for cover and will walk and feed along its edges. One of my favorite tricks is to look for high ground in a lowland area, such as a narrow strip of dry land between swamps or lakes. Whitetails love water and the thick cover that swamps offer, but when they're going from Point A to Point B they will almost always look for the easiest route, and high ground is it. In fact, I cannot think of a single time I have gone looking for a strip of high ground when I did not find an ancient deer trail on it, usually so old that generations of deer hooves have cut a rutted path. These trails are often still evident even if bad winters or limited food have reduced the deer herd in recent years.

If the land you are hunting is relatively flat, most deer still gravitate toward the highest ground, no matter how slight the rise. Any long, low ridge is likely to have a deer trail on it. If a hunter is searching for deer sign and walking quickly along a logging road, he is almost certain to find a deer trail crossing the road at any slight increase in elevation.

The edge where a clearcut borders big timber is a sure bet to have a deer trail running along it because deer, by nature, like edges — the big timber yields easier walking and cover, but the clearcut offers food. Mostly-open, meandering creek bottoms usually have some kind of grassy or brushy growth, but find a wooded finger that crosses it and you will probably find a deer trail.

I really like to set up stands near areas of dense conifer cover, what some would call "dark timber." Whether it is a high ground, jackpine-studded bedding area or a swamp packed with

This 8-pointer tried crossing a low saddle to escape a drive. The author was posted on that very spot.

A black spruce swamp is pinched between two ridges. The near ridge has seen recent logging and the far ridge is covered with oaks. Such a spot deserves a hunter's full attention.

cedars or spruce, a big buck is much more likely to be on his feet during the day in such areas.

Large river bottoms often have trails that follow the edges of not only the river, but the top of the hill above the river. While deer can easily cross a river, if you find a shallow spot where they can walk, rather than swim, to get across you will most likely have a great stand location.

One year I placed a ladder stand in a balsam fir where a partially-frozen river swung tight to the hillside. Knowing the deer probably would not want to deal with the thickening-but-uneven ice, I figured that any traversing the bottomland would eventually work their way to where I waited. Even though the air temperature was 10 degrees below zero when I walked to the stand, I did not have to wait long (nor get too cold) before I filled my tag. I would probably still be hunting this stand if other circumstances didn't make it hard to reach without possibly spooking the deer I hoped to hunt.

As mentioned, ice can restrict deer movement but the thicker it gets the more comfortable they will be with it. A beaver pond that freezes over may not have the funneling effect that it had before it froze, especially when snow on the ice provides better footing. One deer season while hunting from my northern Wisconsin camp, I distinctly remember being told while I was being posted for a drive that I need not watch to my left because of a beaver pond the deer "won't want to cross." About 10 minutes after the other standers marched off to take their places, I scanned the woods and spotted a buck picking its way on the beaver pond, walking directly toward me. I dropped him on the spot, and as he kicked his last he still lay on the ice he was not "supposed" to cross.

I consider it very good to find rubs and scrapes in a funnel area that I am considering hunting. As some would say, "hunt the sign." Rubs and scrapes are signs to deer and are placed in locations where deer travel. I get that, but I do not look to base my decisions for stand sites on what some hunters call rublines. Too often I find rubs where topography has influenced the deer's direction of travel, so that is why I concentrate on funnels first. If the funnel contains lots of buck sign and I can find a spot downwind where I can sit undetected, well, I have found a stand that is probably worth hunting.

I do not like to choose my stands based on what the deer are eating — except when there is a big acorn crop — because in the northwoods they eat just about everything. One must consider hunting in the oaks or very close by when acorns are dropping. However, in most years, there really will not be a preferred food source unless baiting is prevalent where you hunt. And bedding cover? While they favor certain areas — bucks really like high spots where they can easily see or smell approaching danger and readily escape down the hillside or back over the hill — I have seen deer bed in almost every forest type. If they feel safe at the moment and, I guess, are tired, they will lie down in surprisingly open areas. Usually, deer will prefer an area where thicker cover almost forces a predator to make noise, but this isn't always the case. Therefore, if you cannot be sure where they are sleeping or where they are going, you must hunt them where topography influences or forces them to walk. Rubs, scrapes, tracks and droppings confirm that deer are using the route you are considering.

My final search is for the easiest access. I don't want it to be too easy, meaning that I may see other hunters, but I do not want it too difficult, so that walking in or out in the dark is hazardous, or I may alert the resident deer. Old logging roads are priceless, as are tiny, lightweight headlamps with LED lighting to illuminate the way.

CONSIDER WIND

You may find the best deer stand but if you do not account

Deer will use funnel areas for years. The author inspects a rub within range of a stand site he has hunted on and off for nearly 20 years.

for the wind and how it will betray your presence, you may as well not bother to hunt. Like many, I wear scent-blocking clothes and try to stay as odor-free as possible, but if the wind is blowing from where I am sitting toward where I expect the deer to be, it is going to be a long, unproductive wait.

Since the prevailing wind in fall in the north-woods is from the north-west, I choose stand locations that are to the southeast, east or south of the area I intend to watch. In recent years I have preferred stands to the east (west-facing) because easterly winds are less common than those from the south at that time of year.

I consider wind direction far more important

Deer aren't the only ones to look for easy travel. Often logging roads are cut into the woods in the same funnel areas. This logging road is on a strip of high ground between a lake and a dense swamp. Such logging roads can yield access for hunters.

than cover around my stand. Whether I am in a tree or on the ground and sitting completely still, a buck will have a hard time picking me out as it meanders through the forest. It is far easier to fool a deer's eyesight than its sense of smell, which will beat you every time.

CONSIDER COVER

My favorite stand sites have me so well concealed the deer do not know I am there until it is too late. If sitting on the ground, I prefer at the very least to have a large tree at my back to break up my outline, and sitting among the branches of a fallen tree can be a perfect natural ground blind. A sheet of camouflage cloth clothes-pinned to surrounding brush is inexpensive yet can further hide you.

Pop-up "tent" ground blinds and tree stands can be a tremendous aid to a northwoods hunter, but be sure you know the local regulations before you use one or the other. For example, pop-up blinds often require a blaze orange covering, and in many locations neither pop-ups nor tree stands can be left in the woods overnight. Despite these drawbacks, ground blinds can be extremely effective and thanks to their lightweight construction, are extremely portable. Set up a folding bag chair inside and you can comfortably hunt all day from one. Need to stretch

Kevin Schmidt took this buck as it chased a doe past his stand in a funnel area.

your legs or eat a sandwich? As long as you are careful to not brush against the inside of the blind, you can do so without alerting deer. Pop-up blinds can also help contain your scent somewhat on days when the wind is swirling. On the downside, deer readily notice ground blinds so you should set them up days or weeks before you hunt to let the deer grow accustomed to their presence, or "brush them in" by further camouflaging them with natural foliage. However, if it is not legal to leave stands in place overnight where you're hunting, such a blind may be more hindrance than help.

Some hunters like to build ground blinds from fallen trees, stacking them up log cabin-style. While these can be effective, they are also a tip-off to another hunter that the location is a good place to hunt deer. When I am done hunting a spot for a season, I prefer to leave no sign that anyone has ever hunted from that location ... well, nothing outside of a buck's gutpile, which will be cleaned up by scavengers or predators within days. If you build a log cabin-style blind on a spot you like to hunt, you could find another hunter using it next season. Not everyone is considerate of their fellow hunters. Whenever I find such blinds, I check to see if they have had recent use, and if they have, I look for a stand location elsewhere. Such signs of use could be as simple as leaves and/or pine needles being cleared from the inside of the blind, to trash that some leave in the woods. Sometimes you will find fresh cuttings where shooting lanes have been opened. Now, if the stand is covered with pine needles and leaves, and the crossed logs have fallen into disrepair, then I know that the stand has not been used in a couple years. If I see no other sign of hunters I have no problem hunting in that area.

I really like hunting from a ladder tree stand. I look for a spruce, balsam or, at the very least, a white pine with a couple low branches, so I can tuck the seat of the stand and myself in among the branches. Such a location renders a stand-hunter nearly invisible. If I have to break off dead limbs in order to affix the ladder stand to a tree, the strong scent of evergreens helps mask my odor. However, ladder stands tend to be heavy and awkward, and need to be set up in advance. Again, on public land, you may not be able to leave the stand out overnight. A hang-on stand with climbing sticks is also good, but I find ladder stands much more secure. On many public lands it is often illegal to cut live branches to facilitate stand placement or open shooting lanes.

Lightweight climbing tree stands afford mobility and may be your only option on public lands where you are required to remove a tree stand at the end of the day. Unfortunately, they are noisy and require a straight tree trunk to access a tree. Unless your outline is broken by the branches of surrounding trees, too often you are just a readily-noticeable blaze orange or camouflage blob hanging from the tree.

Never use a tree stand — ladder, hang-on or climbing — without a safety harness. Your life may depend on it.

Regardless if I am sitting on the ground or in a tree stand, I wear a camouflage face mask. I am amazed at how many more deer I see from stands since I began wearing a mask. A human face is more visible to deer than many realize.

Finding a good deer hunting stand need not be difficult, though finding a perfect stand is a different story. Homework, and then time in the woods, will reveal great deer funnels. Place your stand downwind of a funnel containing lots of deer sign, and you should be in business.

LAST ALL DAY IN YOUR DEER STAND

"Got a sweet tooth bothering you?" the lady at the mega-mart asked me as she scanned my discounted bag of post-Halloween candy bars.

"Nope. I need these for hunting," I replied because, after all,

I did.

The woman behind the counter eyed me skeptically as she rang up my other items, most of which — she apparently failed to notice — had something to do with hunting. That's okay, because if she asked me why candy bars figure into my hunting plans she probably would not have understood anyway.

My hunting buddies already know what the clerk suspected. I take particular, and perhaps disturbing, pride in hunting a deer stand all day without leaving. Lasting from dawn until dusk is a test of mental and physical endurance, no doubt, but white-tailed deer outfitters from the northern tier of states into Canada would agree that their most successful customers are the ones who stay put once the guide leaves them in their stand.

And why not? Few hunters can move as quietly as a deer, so any time you are up and moving you are disturbing the woods, possibly disrupting the habits of the giant buck that was just around the corner of the trail before you got up to move. But if you are silently watching the woods from a deer stand, its inhabitants soon forget you are even there, which is precisely what a hunter should be trying to achieve.

Regardless of how cold it gets, or how little deer activity the day seems to be producing, I am not leaving my stand. Unless I am just going hunting for a few hours after work, I will stay in my stand from before light until the end of shooting hours — unless I need to tag a buck. Almost all of my biggest bucks have been taken from a stand. I chose the stand location because of a funnel that concentrated deer activity in the area, so this is the absolute best place for me to hunt. Why should I leave?

Lasting all day requires mental toughness, and how one reaches that mindset is up to the individual hunter. Some read while sitting in their stands, others plug in an earphone and listen to a game, some play video games or text with friends, but none of that is for me. I watch the woods and train my focus on

Kevin Schmidt killed this heavy-beamed 8-pointer after hunting from dawn until dusk for five days straight. He shot the buck on the sixth day of the hunt.

every rustle in the leaves or snap of a twig.

WARMTH EQUALS COMFORT

I think the most important factor to hunting the entire day comes down to comfort, and staying warm and dry requires planning. The next few paragraphs will outline how I dress for a day of cold weather hunting; staying warm during the more moderate months does not require as much planning.

I start with a base layer of compression-fitting long underwear. The compression fit promotes blood circulation, and the ability of these high-tech skivvies to wick moisture away from your skin is unrivaled. You will never last all day if the layer next to your skin is damp and clammy. Good riddance to those old cotton union suits!

My second clothing layer involves scent control. The moisture-wicking ability of scent-containing clothing can vary and tends to be delayed, at best, so it is even more important to take your time and not get sweated up while walking to your stand. Some will say that scent-controlling clothing is not necessary if you pay attention to wind direction. Well, I have always played the wind and since I began using scent-controlling clothing I have killed most of my biggest bucks, including the two largest at the time of this writing and three of my four biggest. I will not be without it. My set of scent-containing clothing includes insulated pants and pullover top.

My third layer is a heavyweight fleece shirt that contains a wind-stopping layer, and heavy Malone-style wool pants. I prefer fleece on top for its warmth, quietness and wicking ability, but wool gets the nod for my legs because it provides greater protection than fleece against briars, burdocks and the like. Both will remain warm if they get wet.

If it is really cold I will don a second heavy fleece shirt or light wool jacket, but otherwise my next layer is a heavy camouflage parka, which I roll up and stuff in a backpack for the walk to my stand. To remain safe during gun-hunting season, I wear a blaze orange vest over the fleece shirt or wool jacket, and after I get to my stand I don the parka and pull the vest over the top. The vest contains everything I need at my fingertips — an extra clip loaded with four cartridges, cellphone, and those bite-size candy bars. These treats not only quickly increase my metabolism and help me keep warm, but they provide a mental pick-me-up when not much is happening at my stand. Just take them out of their wrappers and place inside a "zip-lock" plastic bag to minimize noise.

Among other items, I wear waterproof boots with 2,000 milligrams of Thinsulate insulation over a pair of heavyweight, wicking socks. I prefer Thinsulate-lined camouflage glomitts (half glove, half mitten) over my hands because I can keep the fingers together for warmth yet instantly flip the mitten part off when a deer is approaching. I believe camouflage, or at least dark-colored mittens or gloves, are important because any movement you make will be less noticeable to a deer you have not yet seen.

On my head, I pull on a camouflage, scent-containing headcover, then wear a waterproof blaze orange cap over that if gun-hunting. Not only will the headcover control odor, but it insulates the face and neck, and keeps my shiny face from spooking deer. I never go deer hunting without a facemask for these reasons — bow-hunting or gun-hunting.

OTHER EQUIPMENT

I've already mentioned that I use a backpack to carry my heavy parka to my stand, and I carry other all-day essentials in it as well. A sandwich provides energy and a bottle of water prevents dehydration, something which also can cause a hunter to become chilled.

Another inexpensive way to increase warmth is with chemical hand-warmers. One in each mitten or pocket will keep your hands toasty, and you can always stuff one in your boots to thaw cold toes. You can also stuff them into shirt pockets or pin them to your long underwear to help warm your body. Larger warming packs with adhesive backing can be affixed to your long underwear over your chest and your kidneys to help you last even longer. I use these only on extremely cold days, attaching them to my clothing as I get dressed in the morning.

You cannot last all day if you are not comfortable in your stand. If hunting from a ground blind, I sit in a folding bag chair which can be remarkably comfortable. To level your chair, carry a couple 6x6-inch pieces of half-inch plywood in the chair's bag, and place them under the feet of the chair as needed. If hunting from a metal ladder stand, a closed-cell foam pad will conform to your natural shape as well as that of what you are sitting on, and provide an additional layer of insulation. I carry this to my stand in my backpack.

Some hunters use thermal body suits that zip over their hunting clothing. When hunting from ground stands on really cold days, I have occasionally taken an old, canvas sleeping bag with me into the woods. Leave your boots on, step into the bag, pull it up as far as it will go (usually to my armpits), and then put your heavy parka on over the top so it covers the sleeping bag's opening. You will be amazed at much longer a sleeping bag will allow you to hunt without getting cold. If the thermal body suits work that well or better, a stand hunter should consider the purchase.

Eventually, nature will call every hunter, and if you leave your stand to urinate, pay attention to how long it takes the birds, squirrels and deer to resume their habits — by leaving your stand you have disrupted their routine and spread what is likely an unwelcome scent in the woods. (Some hunters believe the odor of human urine is not offensive to deer and may actually attract them, but I have never felt the need to test the theory.) I carry a plastic relief bottle in my backpack and empty it when I am well away from my stand as I leave the woods at the end of shooting hours. My wife considers this habit somewhat disgusting, but doing so limits unwanted noise and, likely, scent.

STAYING SHARP

You can dress warm and follow all the steps outlined above and, eventually, you are still going to get cold. Isometric exercises do not require any movement that will be spotted by a deer, but keep your blood flowing. When I feel like I am on the verge of shivering, I start doing isometrics until the need to shiver has passed. I try to clench the muscles in my torso, neck, legs and arms at the same time and hold for a 15- or 20-count before relaxing. A handful of these will do the job.

It is also hard to be comfortable if you do not feel safe in your stand. Never use a tree stand unless you are wearing a safety harness. Chances are good you will not fall, but peace of mind keeps you focused on the hunt.

You may have spent considerable effort choosing your stand and were convinced of its potential when dawn broke on Opening Day, but when gunshots are ringing in the distance and you are not seeing deer it is easy to second guess yourself. I remind myself that leaving my stand and going for a walk will accomplish nothing, especially since I am wearing the bulky clothes and boots required of a stand-hunter. There was good reason I have chosen this stand and leaving it will diminish my chance of success, and probably increase the odds of other hunters if I spook deer toward them.

The neat thing about stand-hunting is a deer may show at any time. I try to minimize movement completely by scanning the woods around me by moving only my eyes. Once, years ago, I was picked off by a buck 45 yards away through the brush when I spotted movement and turned my head a little too quickly — and I was wearing a camouflage facemask! The buck made the fatal mistake of trotting nervously instead of bolting for safety, and as I affixed my tag to its antlers I realized just how lucky I had been.

One movement that I will allow myself is to reach up and pinch the sides of my nose when I feel a sneeze building (if you don't believe that this works, try it at home before hunting). Deliberately reaching for my nose with camouflage handgear is much less obtrusive than a sudden sneeze, no matter how well you think you suppressed it.

I try to stay sharp mentally by reliving past deer hunting success. In my mind, I envision the last few steps of any bucks I may have killed previously on the stand at which I am sitting, or if I have never tagged a deer from that stand I think of some of my better bucks taken elsewhere as they walked into range. I may try to count how many deer I have taken on that particular

This buck was the 15th the author saw during a week of dawn-to-dusk sits.

day of the hunting season. (I have killed more bucks on the second day of the season than I have on Opening Day, as well as more on the second day of an out-of-state hunt than the first ... I have no idea why.)

As a writer, I will mentally outline articles that I plan to write in the future. I really would rather not think about working when I am hunting, but I have found it remarkably fruitful to take a step back from the office or my computer keyboard and think through a problem while in the relaxing confines of a deer blind.

One of the joys of stand-hunting is the wildlife you see. Watching owls, grouse and other birds, or mammals, as they go about their daily routine is fascinating. I have had chickadees land on my rifle's barrel and the broadhead of my arrow, and the top of my cap or headcover while stand-hunting. I have also seen every animal common to the northwoods from a deer stand. I know of no other way to enjoy such close encounters.

One year, while hunting in Canada with an outfitter, my buddy Kevin and I never left our stands through five and a half days of watching the woods. Snow ... wind ... cold ... 60 degrees one day, you name it, we saw it from tree stands as well as ground blinds. We each saw more than 70 deer, including more than a dozen bucks apiece. Finally, on the sixth and final day, we each killed a buck less than an hour apart. While my buck was the largest I'd seen all week, I had to make a snap decision and, unfortunately, misjudged him ... but he was delicious.

Then, and only then, after nearly six days of dawn-to-dusk vigils, did we leave our stands. It was an extreme test of endurance, but I have been known to do just about anything for a buck.

The author called this 10-pointer within range with a grunt tube.

DEER CALLS AND COMMON SCENTS

My wristwatch revealed that it was 8:30. Even though daylight was about two hours old and I had confidence in the stand I was hunting, I had yet to see a deer. For no other reason than to try to make something happen, I slowly unzipped my parka, reached inside, and slid out the grunt tube that hung from a lanyard around my neck.

Braaaaap! Brrr-brrr-raaaaap! Braaaaap! my call belched over the corner of the grown-up clearcut my stand overlooked. I paused for a minute or so and repeated the call, then put it back inside my coat.

As my eyes scanned to my left, there at the woods' edge stood a nice buck, seemingly bristling for a fight. Steam clouds shot from its nostrils as it breathed and surveyed the scene, and I remember thinking the buck had a lot of points. I eased my rifle into position and hoped the buck would turn to its right to give me a broadside shot. Instead, it stepped stiff-legged straight into the brush that was starting to choke out the decade-old cutting.

With no snow it was hard to follow the buck's progress through the thicket, but occasionally I spotted a flicker of white from its tail or the edge of an ear. When it seemed to disappear, I pulled the call out again and gave it three or four drawn-out notes, and the buck responded by continuing his hunt for the buck he thought was intruding on his territory. I picked him up in my scope, and when I realized that I had a clear view of his chest I touched off the shot.

Instantly the buck dug for the safety of the nearby woods. I followed him through the scope but he disappeared into the timber before my crosshairs lined up again, so I slipped my safety into the "on" position, checked for my knife and rope, and headed toward where he was standing when I squeezed the trigger. There I found a handful of hair, but more importantly, a spray of blood in the brush.

The trail was easy to follow and not long. A short distance inside the timber I spotted an antler branching up from behind a tree root. The tips of his tines were rubbed ivory-white, contrasting strongly with the chocolate color of the rest of his 10-point rack. Immediately I understood why he appeared to have a lot of points when I first saw him.

Almost exactly a year later, hunting a different stand, noon had come and gone with only the sighting of a doe with her twin fawns. Again trying to make something happen, I pulled the grunt tube out and let fly with the funny sound that can be music to a big buck's ears. Five minutes later an 11-pointer showed up and he, too, eventually took a ride home with me in my pick-up truck.

Stories like this would make it seem that calling bucks with a grunt tube is a sure thing, but nothing could be further from the truth. To the right deer, calls and scents can work almost magically, but the problem is finding that deer.

DEER CALLS

There are three types of deer calls popular with hunters today — grunt tubes, bleat (can) calls, and rattling horns or bags. I have used all three in the northwoods with varying and inconsistent success. I presume such calls are more useful and effective in areas with higher concentrations of deer, but the biggest problem with using such calls in the northwoods is there needs to be a buck close enough to hear them.

That said, I will not enter the woods from the middle of October through November without a grunt tube around my neck. Blind-calling, as described in this chapter's opening anecdotes, seems to be less consistently successful than using a grunt tube to call a buck you have already seen into range. In many cases when I have spotted a buck in the distance, I have been able to get him to respond to a grunt tube.

I have had less success with rattling antlers or bags, but at the right time in the pre-rut they can be very effective. However, a friend whose opinions I value highly says he has rattled in bucks as early as the last couple days of September. When rattling has worked for me, I have used both a grunt tube and rattle bag in sequence — first grunting, trying to imitate a buck issuing a challenge toward another, then waiting a minute or so before breaking into a 2-minute rattling sequence. Following the rattling, I will grunt two or three times with the idea of sounding like the victor of the fight. I have had bucks respond instantly on the run as soon as I began rattling, and I have had them sneak in 10 minutes after I have finished. If nothing responds for 20 minutes I will initiate another grunt-rattle sequence.

Only once have I killed a buck that responded to a can call. Ironically, this occurred on the very same morning after I had talked with another hunter in my deer camp and questioned why I was even bothering to take the call because I had "never had a buck respond to it." Because the rut was still in high gear I placed the call in the pocket of my vest, and within minutes of using it that morning the buck approached from behind. He had the call's origin so well pinned down that he walked right past the base of the tree upon which my stand was hanging; had

I been standing on the ground I could have stuck out a leg and tripped the buck as it walked by. The buck walked about 20 yards past my stand and stopped to look around, revealing enough of his shoulder in doing so that I squeezed off the shot.

Bucks have a remarkable ability to locate the source of a call. For this reason, it is imperative to remain still following use of any type of call. If one was close enough to hear the call, it is very possible that he is now looking for its source. Any ill-timed movement on your part could send him on his way.

A fourth call I use is a simple snort, the *Shooooooosh!* of a spooked deer. I make this sound with my mouth and no manufactured call. When a deer snorts (or blows, as some would say) at you it is because it either doesn't know what spooked it or is trying to warn other deer. I try to imitate the sound and reply every time they snort at me. It does not work all the time, but I have caused the snorting deer to settle down and quit making a racket, and in a couple cases the deer came to my call to check out what it likely perceived was another deer. To date I have not killed a buck with this practice.

COMMON SCENTS

The racks of sporting goods stores hang heavy every fall with doe-in-heat scents for good reason — they work. I will be one of the stores' customers as I buy a bottle or two of fresh scent every year. Again, however, you need to find the right buck. I have seen doe-in-heat scents be effective from the last week of October until almost the third week of November.

While I have had many bucks respond positively to doe-in-heat scent, including my first buck, I learned the most from the third-ever northwoods buck I killed. That season, I hunted all of Opening Day without seeing a deer, but on the way out after shooting hours I checked a communal scrape and found that it had been worked sometime during the day. The scrape was about a hundred yards from my stand and I passed it on my way in and out of the woods, so the signs it had been used by a buck that day were obvious. Fresh grooves had been cut into the earth by a buck's front hoof, and fresh dirt was sprayed onto the leaves. Knowing the local sporting goods store would close soon, I hot-footed it out of the woods and paid for the scent just minutes before the proprietor shut his doors.

Before dawn the next morning I sprayed some of the newly-purchased scent into the scrape, then dribbled it periodically on the leaves toward my stand. About a half-hour after legal shooting light I heard a branch snap in the direction of the scrape and spotted a deer trotting quickly in my direction, its nose inches above the leaves. The antlers were obvious and when the buck presented a shot I dropped him in his tracks.

Doe-in-heat scent dribbled in a scrape and leading to the author's stand brought this buck on the run.

That incident taught me to use scent to spread the effective coverage of my stand beyond what I can see. Scent can grab the attention of bucks that are working an area and lead them within range. While I merely dribbled scent on the forest floor that time, I now use a drag rag to achieve the same results.

An old, white or light gray T-shirt can make a perfect drag rag. I wash the shirt with scent-eliminating clothing soap, then cut most of it away, leaving only a 9- or 10-inch wide strip of cotton attached to the collar. I then place scent on the back end of the shirt and store it in a zippered-top plastic bag. When I have walked to within about a hundred yards of my stand, I put the collar of the old shirt over my boot and around my ankle, and then simply walk to a shooting lane or an open area within range of my stand, the shirt dragging in the leaves behind me and leaving the scent. However, I'll continue on for another hundred yards in the opposite direction, then turn around and return to the shooting lane, where I take the rag off my boot and hang it from a tree or stump about waist-high. Sometimes I add more scent somewhere in the process.

This practice creates a trail of scent that not only leads bucks to my stand but also expands the area where wind can pick up and spread the scent. I believe this is much more effective than merely pouring a few drops of scent in front of your stand. And, the white or light gray shirt hanging at waist height replicates the back end of a doe when seen through the woods; now, I cannot say with certainty that the bucks agree with me, but it does not hurt. When I am ready to leave the woods I take the shirt with me, returning it to the plastic bag. First and foremost the shirt is litter that should not be left in the woods, but it also could be found overnight by a buck who now knows the set-up is fraudulent.

Sometimes a buck will just show up in the area and sometimes they will literally walk down the trail like a hound on scent. I have seen this enough to believe the ten dollars or so that a bottle of doe-in-heat scent costs is easily a worthwhile investment.

Cover Scents

Like many hunters, for years I used skunk scent as a cover scent, believing the foul odor would effectively cover my human odor (which probably smells just as foul to a deer). But then I read somewhere that skunk odor may alert deer because, after all, skunks don't just spray randomly — something bad had to have occurred. Whether a deer can reason enough to make this connection is debatable, but I stopped using skunk scent and did not notice a decrease in the number of deer I was seeing. My nose thanked me.

However, in the seasons leading up to the publication of this book, I have been using a spray cover scent that has a much more pleasant odor — that of vanilla. Deer that have walked downwind of me while I have used this scent certainly notice it. To date, every one has stopped, smelled the air for a while, and then relaxed and gone about its business.

The scent is strong enough that I believe individual deer could become conditioned to it with time, but so far the benefits to the hunter appear substantial. I for one plan to keep using it.

Eric Adams, a hunting camp partner of the author's, was still-hunting along the top of a ravine and shot this 10-pointer as it sneaked along the other side.

On The Move: Still-Hunting & Tracking

Forty yards away in the bottom of the ravine, the back half of a deer stuck out from behind the trunk of a large white pine. And it was not moving.

No matter how hard I peered through my scope, I could not see anything of the front part of the deer. No head, antlers, shoulder or rib cage. The back half was good size, and I figured it had to be a buck. There is no question in my mind that he knew I was there, and to this day I believe he figured that if he could not see me, then I could not see him. That's fine, but the back half was unmistakable ... and not moving.

My rifle grew heavy. Still the buck would not move. Finally, I stomped my foot against the dry leaves a couple times and the deer had to see what was making the commotion. He stepped forward, revealing a nose, then a head with a nice set of antlers, his neck, and finally his chest. I centered the crosshairs on his rib cage, pulled the trigger, and within minutes was admiring the only buck to date that I have killed while still-hunting or tracking on completely dry ground.

Why I wanted to still-hunt that day escapes me. The woods were brown and dry, and there was no way to avoid a steady *crunch-crunch-crunch* while moving. So, I decided to try to sound like a deer or a squirrel moving through the leaves. I would take three or four quick, short steps, then pause to look around. I made no effort to stay quiet because there was no way I could. And it worked.

Few deer hunters are not intrigued by still-hunting or tracking, methods in which a hunter pits his skills of sneaking through the woods against the hyperactive senses of the white-tailed deer. Perhaps it appeals to the romantic side in deer hunters, who relish the thought of going one-on-one with the deer. For 10 years I tried my best to become an expert still-hunter, but when I realized I was not killing the kind of bucks I wanted, I went back to stand-hunting. Maybe my Lasik-improved eyesight is not good enough, or maybe I am just too big of a guy to move with the necessary stealth. Maybe I should have kept going a few more years and the necessary skills would have developed.

Still, I have killed a number of bucks and some does while still-hunting, and once tracked down a buck that I had missed from a stand earlier in the day and killed him as he rose from his bed. Maybe I would be more successful on the move if the country where my deer camp is located was anything but flat and thick, where a 50-yard shot is a long one. Maybe I would be more successful if fresh snow was a more common occurrence during the hunting season at my camp. This chapter is what I know about a hunting technique at which few are consistently successful.

HUNT BIG COUNTRY

You cannot go one-on-one with the deer where there are dozens of other hunters in the woods. High numbers of hunters disrupt normal deer movement and patterns. To be most successful as a still-hunter or tracker, you need deer that are going about their daily lives as if a deer season was not occurring. Skittish deer are best hunted from stands overlooking escape routes or topography that funnels their movement. If you try still-hunting in these conditions you will be, at best, acting as a "driver," keeping the deer moving for the stand-hunters.

To find big country in the northern states, obtain a topographic map, study it, and buy a good compass and learn how to use it, and you should be set. You can take this a step further by buying a GPS and downloading topographical maps to it. Carry the map, GPS and compass with you in the woods and you should not have to worry about getting lost. If you plan to hunt where private lands abut public acreage, be sure you know the boundaries in advance. Commercial downloadable GPS maps or cellphone apps are available with private land boundaries indicated, and can be a tremendous help.

It is also best to use land contours to your advantage. Hunting along the top of a ravine or ridge allows you to scan downhill and better see into the cover than if you hunt level terrain, where the cover tends to blend together a short distance away and limits your range of visibility.

I choose to hunt in areas similar to those I would select for stand-hunting. Natural landforms funnel deer movement. Since you are going to the deer, it is smart to go where they already are or eventually will be.

LET THE TACTIC DICTATE YOUR SPEED

If you are still-hunting, moving too quickly is the biggest mistake you can make. For the most part, the deer you are hunting are undisturbed and either bedded or browsing, and if you move too quickly they will spot you first. Then, they will most likely lay low and let you walk past, or take off in thunderous fashion.

A good still-hunting speed can only be measured by the woods and the animals in it. If you are seeing grouse on the ground and getting close before they flush or they merely cluck and wander off, if squirrels and chickadees are moving about and not shutting up, then you are moving at the right speed. One must travel without causing a disturbance. It helps to pick your feet up when stepping, rather than shuffling. With each step I place my foot down slowly, feeling for anything brittle beneath before putting my weight on it.

Try to move fluidly through the woods, regardless if still-hunting or tracking. Slow, methodical, fluid movements are less noticeable than fast, jerky action. When you stop, try to do so alongside a large tree to break your outline. Try to limit the movement of your hands.

Tracking will often require that you move quickly through the woods. If you take a large, fresh buck's track and the animal is walking in a relatively straight line with a good stride between hoofprints, you had better sling your rifle and try to exceed his pace; otherwise, the buck will seldom be caught. Walk alongside his tracks, rather than in them, because doing so would obliterate the only connection between the hunter and hunted.

The hunter should watch the buck's sign as he follows. If the buck joins up with a doe and begins chasing, follow quickly because both animals will be preoccupied. When his tracks begin to meander and he stops to browse, it is time to slow down and hunt more with your eyes than your feet. A meandering, browsing buck will soon be a bedded buck, and he may be close. Try to spot him first before he decides to run.

This is precisely what happened when I tracked down the buck that I had missed from my stand earlier in the day. After my errant shot, I saw by his tracks in the snow that the buck initially ran, then slowed to a trot within a hundred yards. Soon he joined a doe, and they headed toward a known bedding area not far away. I was on the edge of the bedding area when I noticed both deer had begun feeding on hazelbrush buds. The two deer lay down lots of tracks in a very small area as they fed on the tiny buds, and pieces of hazelbrush lay atop the snow. I instantly began hunting with my eyes more than my feet. About 10 minutes later I heard a pop and I turned to my left to see the buck starting to rise. My shot took him through the heart.

HUNT WITH YOUR EYES

My good friend and deer campmate Paul Ratliff gave me the best piece of advice years ago when I started to learn how to poke and mosey (as they call it in my camp). "Too many guys spend too much time looking at their feet and the ground, trying to pick the most quiet route to walk," Paul told me. "There are no deer between your eyes and your feet. You need to keep your eyes on the woods in front and to the side of you if you hope to see deer."

When tracking, remind yourself to pick out the direction of the track, but rather than focus solely on the track, look ahead and to the sides. Regardless if the buck is wounded or unscathed, you will never see him if your eyes are only on the track. Rather than looking ahead at eye level into the woods, look to where the trees and ground meet. You will spot more bedded deer that way and be better prepared to shoot when one does get up to run.

"Don't worry about occasionally breaking a stick as that's a natural sound in the woods," Paul continued. "If you do break a stick, pause for a moment and see what happens before continuing, but keep your eyes on the woods." Since I have size 13 feet I probably need to be more conscious about being quiet than Paul. I have found a happy medium — I quickly glance downward for sticks or other noisemakers, plan my steps, direct my eyes back on the woods and walk the pre-planned steps. I then pause to scan the surrounding terrain, then repeat the process.

Still, deer are not the easiest things to spot in the woods unless there is a substantial snow cover. Without snow, the gray/brown of a deer's coat matches the forest floor quite well. Throw in the typically sullen, cloudy days of November, and it is even harder to discern gray/brown from brown. Therefore, it is good to carry a pair of quality optics for a quick, safe check of anything that looks suspiciously like a deer. The new binocular harnesses that cross your back and put their weight on your torso, rather than your neck, are one of the best investments a hunter can make.

One year, my eyes told me a buck was standing under some balsams — I had its antlers, ears, neck and front shoulder picked out from the surrounding brush. When I checked it with the binocs, however, the "shoulder" and "neck" became a stump, and the "antlers" and "ears" became branches well behind the stump. I was dumbfounded — I looked again without the binocs and could see what I thought was the buck, then checked the area thoroughly again with the optics and saw the same stump and branches.

You can do the same thing with a riflescope, but for safety reasons it is best to check uncertain targets with binoculars — you do not want to be aiming a rifle at something that may materialize into a fellow hunter.

HUNT WITH YOUR EARS

A major part of knowing what's going on in the woods around you is paying attention to the sounds of the woods. Quite often you will hear a deer approaching long before you see it. Concentrate on sounds in the distance, and try to block your own sound from your consciousness. With time in the woods and concentration, anyone can do this.

Notice the subtle noises of the woods. Slight rustling can be a deer walking somewhere near you. Some of the deer I've killed while still-hunting were heard long before they were seen. At times, if you are quiet enough, you can even hear deer walking in soft snow. Branches clacking together may be a buck rubbing its antlers. A sudden thump could be a deer leaving its bed in a hurry, or stomping its hooves at you or something else it does not like. Tune in to the woods, and tune yourself out.

Hunt The Conditions

Most states have bow-hunting seasons that last for months, rather than the handful of days allotted to gun-hunters, so while a bow-hunter can pick his moments a gun-hunter has to make the best of the conditions at present. Certain conditions are far better than others, of course. In most hunters' minds, the best conditions involve snow — not too much to inhibit walking, and not so little that it is in danger of melting quickly on a somewhat warm day. In this idyllic world, the weather will be slightly overcast and just around freezing, so it is not too uncomfortable and the snow stays quiet and soft. A slight breeze into the face, or crosswind, is preferred.

It does not take many years in the woods for a hunter to understand that the perfect conditions outlined above do not happen very often, but that is okay. On a windy or snowy day, or a mixture thereof, try to sneak through places where you know whitetails like to bed. Wind-blown tree limbs and snow hide your movement, and the sound of the wind rushing through the trees covers the noise you make. Rain does the same thing and makes the woods even quieter, save for the dripping of water onto the forest floor.

As discussed earlier, it is entirely possible to kill a deer on dry ground. However, two conditions that won't work are a wind at your back because any deer ahead of you will have ample warning that you are coming, and crunchy snow. There is no way you can sound like a squirrel on crunchy snow because you weigh so much more and will break through the crust. Even the deer do not like to move much in crunchy snow, especially if they know they are being hunted. If the snow has been melting and there are patches of bare ground between patches of crunchy snow, try to stay on the bare ground as much as possible because it is usually quieter.

Bright, sunny days are not my favorite conditions for still-hunting. Lots of things shine and glare in the sun, from tree bark to deer antlers to the glasses many hunters wear on their face. I try to adjust my hunting plans by taking both the sun and the wind into account, trying to keep the wind in my face and the sun at my back when walking through the best areas. Naturally, that is not always possible.

DRESS FOR SUCCESS

Good still-hunters do not dress the same as good stand-hunters. You must plan your hunting outfit, from your head to your feet. Remember, you are moving through the woods, and it is best to think light — try still-hunting in a blaze orange snowmobile suit (which may work perfectly well for a stand-hunter) and you will see what I mean.

On my head I like to wear an uninsulated blaze orange cap that will not trap heat and will not get snagged by brush and snatched from my head like a knit cap. For pants, I prefer light-weight wool, which is quiet yet warm, even when wet. Wool also protects your legs from briars and other brush better than any other material used to make pants. I used to wear a wool shirt but now prefer heavyweight fleece with some kind of wind-cutting lining. This too is ultra-quiet, warm when wet, and dries quickly. Underneath I wear high-tech, compression long underwear, which wicks away moisture. On top I wear a wool jacket, which is warm when wet, breathes well, and very quiet. Over that I wear a blaze orange vest which has ample pockets for extra shells, drag rope, compass, map, sandwich, candy bars and a bottle of water, without having to use a fanny pack.

For boots, nothing beats Gore-Tex for light weight and breathability, with 200 to 400 milligrams of Thinsulate insulation. Some of today's new boots designs fit like a tennis shoe, weigh only slightly more, provide great ankle support, and have a tread on the bottom that provides sure footing in slippery conditions.

FURTHER READING

If you desire more information about still-hunting and tracking, here are five books that are must-reads and well worth their price:
- *Hunting Big Woods Bucks, Vols. 1 & 2*, by Hal Blood
- *How To Bag The Biggest Buck Of Your Life*, by Larry Benoit
- *Big Bucks The Benoit Way*, by Bryce Towsley
- *Whitetail*, by George Mattis

The author's son, Brant, killed his largest buck as it tried to sneak into a river bottom ahead of a drive.

BIG WOODS
DEER DRIVES

Four or five days into the gun deer season and you can read the handwriting on the wall. The deer stand that once was so promising in the buildup to Opening Day has fizzled, and only does, fawns, and a single small buck have wandered past — and even he was nothing more than a ghost in the brush. Making things worse, fewer gunshots echo over the hillsides with each passing day.

Many hunters will point an accusing finger at bait piles or timber wolves or the DNR or the weather or the rut coming to an end. They may complain about the wind not being right for their favorite stand. Regardless, frustration and self-doubt build while the days count down.

Do you give up? Maybe hunt another morning or two, but quit early in the afternoon? To me, unfilled tags have a bitter taste, and a bowl of tag soup is the last thing I want at season's end. So, if the deer will not come to me, I figure it is time to go to them. The members of the northern Wisconsin hunting camp to which I belong look forward to the days following Thanksgiving because we know someone in our ranks may have a chance at a big buck. But you do not need to limit yourselves to the final days of the season because a properly-executed deer drive will work anytime, from season's open to close.

The art of driving deer has largely been forgotten by today's deer hunter. Maybe it is because of increasingly fractionalized private woodlots, or maybe a whole generation of hunters prefers tree stands. Certainly hunting camps are smaller on average than in years gone by. Most hunters just do not try to push deer anymore. Still, our crew, usually numbering fewer than 10 hunters, takes on the challenge of driving big woods with gusto. When deer are not moving, whether because of the weather, the close of the rut, hunting pressure, or only-God-knows-what, it is time to make drives. You have to buy into the concept that individually your chances are not very good, but collectively, be there two hunters or 20 in your group, your odds will be better.

Know your local deer hunting regulations before you make drives. Wisconsin allows "group" deer hunting, and a hunter may tag a deer shot by another as long as the tag holder is within shouting distance of the shooter. While this may sound trivial, the group deer hunting law legalized what most camps had practiced anyways. It is also important to know property boundaries because you do not want to trespass on land that belongs to others.

DEER DRIVES, IN THEORY

A deer drive works by having "drivers" walk through the woods toward the locations where other hunters, the "standers," are positioned. The drivers move the deer, the standers intercept them. Usually the number of standers will outnumber the drivers, often by a 2-to-1 or 3-to-1 margin. The biggest factor is trying to cover all the known escape routes with standers. Even large parcels can be pushed by two or three drivers if they know the woods and where the deer most likely will be found.

Accept the fact that deer will squirt out in places you did not expect, but that is all part of the game. When everything comes together and a big buck is down, all the frustration of previous drives that did not work will be forgotten.

Paul Ratliff, a hunting camp partner of the author's, shot this giant 11-pointer as it followed a river's edge ahead of a drive.

Every magazine article I have read about driving deer has been replete with drawings of supposedly-magical drives in which the drivers make big circles or play follow-the-leader. These kind of drives may apply in areas of small woodlots, but simply aren't practical in the big woods. And, my camp has never done them, so I am not going to discuss them here. Rather, I am going to explain the subtleties of driving deer and you can take it from there. The diagrams you will find in these pages illustrate how deer tend to react to drives depending on wind direction.

Deer are creatures of habit. As long as there is a favorable food source nearby, most deer will continue to use it and bed in cover nearby. Bucks will come and go as the rut progresses, eventually returning to their home range when breeding ends. However, when pressed, deer will usually take the same escape route their ancestors used. Often this follows the lay of the land, other times it is merely a quick route from where they were spooked to the safety of thick cover. If you find such an escape route, either by clever sleuthing or merely stumbling across it, file it away because the deer will continue to use it for years.

The keys to driving the big woods are similar to the basic tenets of deer hunting — stealth and playing the wind. Stealth means being able to quietly position standers in places you expect the deer to go when pushed, so logging roads and deer trails that allow easier access to stands are important. Standers must minimize noise — talking when discussing plans must be kept to a minimum, and then it must be in hushed tones. Once the standers are in place, their chances of killing a deer begin immediately as they may see a deer moving about on its own, well before the drive begins, or they may spot a deer pushed out by drivers or other standers getting into position. Standers must always stay alert.

As drivers get into position and wait for the standers to assume their places, they must also be quiet because there's nothing

Bucks will use the same escape routes for generations. This 9-pointer by Ryan Adams was shot in the exact location as Paul Ratliff's buck pictured on Page 91.

worse than pushing deer out before the standers are in place. And, occasionally, standers who are getting in position will bump deer in the direction of the drivers. There is no better feeling than when a buck is down before a drive even commences.

Position your standers where low ridges head toward a swamp, where a saddle allows quick access from a hillside bench to a river bottom, where fingers of brush provide cover while going from Point A to Point B ... you get the picture. A great stand is in a ravine where the deer think they can quickly escape the drive, yet the stander(s) can cover a large area because of the advantage that elevation affords. If a strip of big timber bisects a thicket, make sure it is covered by a stander. I am convinced that escaping deer look ahead to big timber for a reference point as they run through thick cover, and bucks with wide racks will often skirt the edge of big timber because it affords easier running.

If legal to do so, install ladder tree stands before the season in the locations where the standers on your drives will later be posted. There are two advantages to getting your standers off the ground — they will cover a greater area, and the shots they take will be safer as they are angled downward. And ladders are a better choice than climbing stands because they allow quicker, quieter access.

THE DRIVE BEGINS

The drive should start at a pre-arranged time. Drivers should walk at a pace similar to taking a simple hike in the woods. Forget what you may have heard about barking or banging pie tins because with that kind of unwanted noise, deer will easily pinpoint the drivers, circle away from them, and lie down. Such disturbances may work fine if there is a large number of drivers, but won't be very effective for a smaller group. If drivers sneak too slowly and with too little noise, deer seem to have a difficult

Ben Cogger killed this 9-pointer as it headed for a swamp along a low ridge ahead of the drivers.

time picking them out so again they simply lie down until the pressure passes. You just about have to "step" on the deer to get them to go in this situation. A steady pace with an occasional pause to look around is a good plan.

That pause while walking is crucial for the drive's success. Often a big buck that is bedded as a drive commences may not make the effort to move if the driver does not walk closely, or "step on them," as the saying goes. Big bucks are old bucks, and it is possible they have seen drives before. They seem to know that if they run they become vulnerable, and they probably chose their current bedding area because they felt safe, so that is where they're going to stay. But then a driver pauses ... we have no idea what a buck is thinking when this happens, but it is possible they believe they have been spotted. The longer you wait, the greater the test of the buck's nerves. How long should you pause before resuming your walk? Wait at least a 10-count, but if you are in an area from which you have pushed out bucks before, a 20-count is not out of the question. You cannot wait much longer because you still have a drive to make and you need to try to keep up with the other drivers, but they should be pausing occasionally, too, so this is not that big of an issue.

Drivers should always keep their eyes up, off the ground, and looking around as they walk. Quite often the deer will not run toward the standers but will go across the drive, and the buck you jump may be shot by one of the other drivers. Drivers should carry a GPS or, at the very least, flagging ribbon to mark where they have shot a deer. Make sure the deer is down, tag it and mark its location, and resume the drive because others are counting on you.

A GPS can be useful in the hands of every driver. True, many who have hunted for years can probably make a successful drive either by simply "knowing" the drive from past efforts, by watching the treeline, or by using a compass. However, many drives

Ben Cogger's buck was driven out of a known deer bedding area. The buck dressed at 210 pounds, and carried antlers that were broken from fighting.

will be made by people who do not have the same experience. The "new blood" of a camp needs to learn sometime. A GPS with pre-loaded maps can instantly show a driver where he is in a drive, and if the positions of the standers are already marked with waypoints, the drive will become much more precise as the drivers will come out right at the stands.

While walking, drivers should always poke through known bedding cover. Usually this is the thickest cover in the drive — either grass, brush or evergreens — but it can often be the tops of ridges or hogsbacks, or a flat overlooking a river or creek bottom. One drive we make has a hillside bench where deer like to overlook a river bottom, and I have stood in the exact same spot more than a dozen times while standers in the river bottom were shooting at deer. This drive requires the drivers to walk in a southwesterly direction. Midway through the drive I bump into a logging road that runs north-south. I turn north, follow the road to the top of the hill, then step back into the woods and resume my southwesterly route, which is usually when things get exciting because that is where they bed. At times, I have heard the deer run down the hillside, and then counted the seconds until the shooting started.

A camp planning a deer drive must be conscious of the wind. Understand there is no perfect direction to push deer that will work 100 percent of the time, but crosswind or upwind work the best (see the diagrams on Pages 99 and 101).

I believe the single best direction to push deer is crosswind; the fact the most successful drives our camp has made were crosswind probably causes me to think this way. The deer usually won't want to run crosswind completely through the drive and usually turn into the wind at some point, so the standers for such a drive should be positioned in sort of a semi-circle. Some will be crosswind of the drivers' direction, others upwind.

At the start of a crosswind drive the deer usually stay ahead

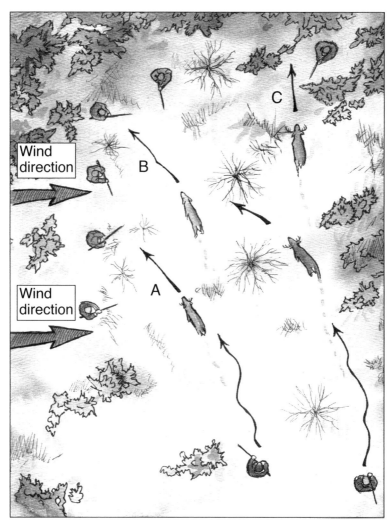

Setting up for a crosswind drive is usually most effective with big woods bucks. The more they're pushed, the more the deer will eventually want to head into the wind so they know what's ahead of them (A). They may hit a stander's scent stream, hesitate, and then veer off where they may run into another stander (B). Though most will head in that direction, some may continue crosswind (C).

of the drivers, seemingly content to know they can bail out into the wind if necessary. They may pick up a stander's scent stream and turn one way or the other; with luck the change of course will lead them to another stander.

A drive that goes directly into the wind requires more effort and/or standers to try to close off the end of the drive. As the drive commences the deer will often head directly into the wind toward the standers, but they usually eventually run into the odor stream of one of the standers and change course. It is remarkable to see their tracks in snow go toward a stander, mill around a bit to assess their next move, and then turn crosswind just out of sight. Often their direction change will be less than 200 yards from the standers' positions. If you don't have standers in crosswind positions the deer will soon be out of the drive and nobody will see them.

If you try to push the deer downwind they'll have the drivers' positions pinpointed immediately and often will just lay low because they really don't like to move with the wind. If they do not simply bed down and let the drivers walk by, they will soon turn crosswind and again, nobody will see them. Occasionally a stander positioned crosswind will see deer, but drives going downwind are essentially handicapped from the beginning.

SAFETY FIRST

When you concentrate a number of hunters in a small area, and a group of them is walking toward the others, the chances of every hunter's nightmare — an accidental shooting — increases. Safety is the foremost concern. Standers and drivers must be absolutely certain of their target when they pull the trigger. It's good to have an experienced hunter serve as a leader as the standers are dropped off. Not only does such a hunter know exactly where the standers should be positioned, but as he does so he should instruct them where other standers will be posted, as

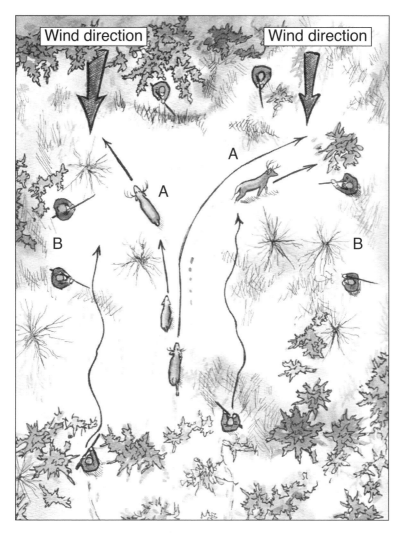

Driving deer into the wind can be very effective because they really like to head that way when pushed or spooked. If they run into the scent streams of the standers, they will likely veer off crosswind (A). Therefore, it's important to have standers positioned crosswind of the direction you're trying to move the deer (B). It's more important to have more standers than drivers to intercept them where they try to sneak out of the drive.

Paul Ratliff took this 8-point, 220-pound buck as it tried to sneak out of a tag alder swamp ahead of a drive.

well as where and when they can expect to see the drivers.

Our camp has a firm rule that standers never leave their posts until the drivers are out, regardless if they have shot at a buck. There could be more deer coming, and a moving stander may spook these animals and ruin his own chances as well as those of the other standers. More important, however, a situation in which a stander wanders in areas where others do not expect him could end horribly. Blaze orange does wonders for hunter safety, but its brilliance can still be swallowed up quickly by thick woods.

Deer driving is such a lost art that generations of the animals may never have tried to sneak out of one. If the deer are not coming to you, go to them for a day or two and see what happens.

The author's bullet blew up inside the chest cavity of this huge 8-pointer, necessitating a tracking job that was more difficult than it should have been.

THE SHOT:
BEFORE & AFTER

All too often when we hunt deer, the buck just appears without prior warning. You had been watching intently, or maybe even dozing, and all of a sudden a buck is in your shooting lane. That is where I found myself that November morning.

I had booked a hunt with a Canadian outfitter that year, and the stand where he placed me overlooked an ATV trail that crossed a funnel area. Big woods were pinched down between a steep ridge and a plowed hayfield. "The bucks like to come out of the timber in the morning and head for the black spruce swamp you'll see to your left," he told me. As is the custom when deer hunting in Canada, corn had been dumped as bait about 50 yards away on the ATV trail to lure in does, which in turn will attract rutting bucks. As daylight grew I could see the week-old snow was cut in all directions by deer hooves. About 20 yards beyond the bait on the trail was a dark spot, and my binoculars revealed it to be a large scrape.

I settled in for what I thought would be a long day of waiting atop the ladder stand. I may have been dozing, or I may have been looking in another direction, but when my eyes scanned the trail before me the buck was just there, pawing the scrape. I eased my rifle onto the stand's shooting rest and pushed the safety into the "fire" position, and the buck threw its head up and glared at me with that "just who the heck do you think you are?" look that they all do so well.

His antlers sat like a large crown atop his head and extended well beyond his ears, and I knew instantly what I would do. The rifle bucked as soon as the crosshairs settled on his rib cage, and the buck kicked and then sprinted in a death run for the black spruce and disappeared. My watch revealed the time was only 7:15 ... so much for the long day I thought lay ahead of me.

Immediately I unloaded my rifle, climbed down from the stand, shed some heavy clothing, reloaded, and headed out to look for my deer. Arriving where he stood at the scrape, I was surprised to find no sign of a hit — no hair or blood. Looking toward the spruces where the buck had run, there was really no discernible trail because of the old snow and heavy deer traffic in the area.

Well, he disappeared in the spruces, so I might as well walk along the edge of them. There's sure to be blood there, I thought to myself. The spruces were about 75 yards from where the buck stood when I shot, so I circled around to their edge. Again, no blood, but I did find a single, giant, fresh, running track, which I flagged with surveyor ribbon.

I walked back to the scrape and hung surveyor ribbon there, then eyeballed a straight line between the two markings and walked to the spruce. I found a couple more of the large tracks, so I figured I had my buck's exit marked, but I could not find blood nor hair. It appeared as if I had completely missed the buck — a standing shot of about 70 yards, and I had a rest!

Doubt was really starting to set in now, so I climbed back into the ladder stand to see if an unseen branch may have deflected the shot, but the sight picture was clear. I walked back to the scrape and decided to walk to the spruce's edge, eyeball the angle, and plunge into the swamp in the direction the buck had run.

Twenty-five yards into the spruce my heart skipped as I found three small spots of blood soaked into the snow. I looked up, saw more blood, and on the other side of a small balsam lay my buck! He had run about 125 yards from where he had been shot without bleeding until he was about to fall over, and had likely been dead seconds after I pulled the trigger. Upon closer inspection, I discovered my shot had hit the giant 8-pointer precisely where I'd aimed, but there was no exit wound. Later, after gutting the deer, we learned the bullet had blown up on impact. A year later, after I had killed another buck and a bear with the bullets also exploding inside the animals, I switched to a better quality cartridge. But that is another story.

From the time I shot the buck until I found it, nearly an hour and a half elapsed. And this was with a buck that was dead on its feet and did not run very far, and likely dropped within a minute of the shot. How many deer are lost because hunters give up on a trail, or simply cannot find it? The goal of this chapter is to help prevent such unnecessary losses.

SHOOT AT THE FIRST OPPORTUNITY

I am a fan of several of the hunting shows that appear on television. I like the shows that are professionally filmed and focus on the hunt, not on goofball antics. I live vicariously by watching these programs — maybe I do not have the inclination or the resources to go on such a hunt, but I can see what the experience is all about thanks to television. I have even learned a few things. However, such shows can do a disservice to beginning hunters.

Too often the hunter being filmed waits for a perfect, broadside shot, or he waits until his videographer has sufficient footage of the animal before he pulls the trigger on his rifle, muzzleloader, or arrow release. Now, if you are bow-hunting, it is smart to wait for the shot, and a broadside or quartering away angle will result in a short tracking job if you place the arrow where it needs to go. But if you are hunting with a rifle or a muzzleloader, take the first killing shot that presents itself because you may never get a second chance if you wait for a perfect angle.

If I can, I want to shoot a buck through both lungs. Find that notch on its side behind the knee and center the crosshairs halfway between the back and belly, and it is highly unlikely the buck will run more than 50 yards. But this is a perfect world scenario. If the buck is quartering toward or away from you, aim for its opposite shoulder and your shot will likely drop it in its tracks. If it runs, chances are very good that it will not go far.

Mouth-grunting or even yelling at a buck that is on the move can be effective at stopping it for a standing shot. Some hunters will not do this for fear of spooking the buck, but I have stopped several running bucks with this technique. My son was 12 years old and on his first deer hunt, sitting alongside me in a tree, when a 6-point buck came loping along the top of a ridge. I yelled "Maaaaah!" at it and the buck bounded to a stop only 25 yards in front of Brant. He proceeded to miss it cleanly, but that too is another story for another time.

I have only shot a couple of bucks in any location other than the chest. A neck or head shot is very risky because it is a small target that may suddenly move. No matter how hard the deer may drop to the ground, be ready as you approach it because your shot may have only grazed and stunned it.

Regardless of how well I *think* I hit a buck, as long as it is on its feet I keep shooting (if I am able). I would much rather place my tag on a shot-up animal than deal with the disappointment, frustration and guilt of losing a wounded deer that I could have shot again but did not because I had too much confidence in the first shot. Always approach a downed buck cautiously; I do so from behind and touch the deer's eye before I do anything else. If it blinks, it is still alive, so shoot it again. If its eyes are closed, it is also still alive so shoot it again. A dead buck's eyes will be open and usually already fixed by the time you get to the animal.

One of the most unnerving things I have done is to walk up on a nice buck that I had dropped as it ran out of a drive, and then watch the deer pick its head up and look me in the eye as I approached. The buck came out of the drive almost immediately and I hit it hard in the shoulder as it ran in front of me. It hunched up and turned, but kept going. My second and third shots were clean misses, but my fourth, which hit it high in the shoulder, put it down for keeps. It twitched once or twice, but appeared to be finished. When the drivers came out, I left my stand and walked toward the deer, fully expecting it to be dead, but then it lifted its head and glared at me. Though far from my biggest buck, a set of antlers upright at about five paces is something I do not care to see again. Though the buck could not get up to run, I still had to shoot it through the neck to finish it.

There usually is no need to wait before taking the trail after shooting a buck with a rifle or muzzleloader. Unless the deer is shot in the paunch, there is no point in this and may actually keep one from catching up to it. A buck shot through the lungs or heart that runs off will be dead by the time you climb out of your stand, so you might as well take the trail. Only twice have I shot a deer in the paunch and in both cases we took the trail immediately. One was hit so hard it could not run and I ended its ordeal within minutes, and in the other case snow was melting from the trees and obliterating the trail, so we took the track immediately and eventually caught up to the animal and finished it off.

A deer that is hit superficially should be tracked immediately. Often, its first reaction is to bed down due to shock, and a hunter who sneaks up on the buck may be able to finish it off quickly. Once the buck gets its second wind and the shock is gone from its system, it can put a lot of distance with an uncertain blood trail behind it, even while running on three legs.

Of course, all of this is different for a buck shot with an arrow. Broadheads kill deer by hemorrhaging, not by shock as with a bullet, so you need to give a deer time to die. I wait 20 minutes between loosing an arrow and taking the track, and some hunters prefer a 30-minute wait.

BE OBSERVANT

After you shoot, whether it be with a rifle or bow, try to take note of where the deer was hit and watch how the animal reacts. A buck hit in the vitals will almost always run hard. If it kicked its hind legs upward after the shot, it was probably hit in the heart. Bucks that appear to be dragging a front leg have likely been hit in the shoulder and should die soon. A large 8-pointer that I shot with a bow labored to clear small balsams as it ran and I knew seconds after taking the shot the buck would not go far, and he did not.

A buck hit in the paunch will be a dead buck, but you have to let it die. If there is no rain or snow in the forecast, leaving the animal overnight is probably the best choice. If you do not push it, the buck probably will not go far before bedding down, and will likely be dead the next morning. If it is still alive it will be a very sick animal, one you should finish quickly.

When I take a trail, I walk immediately to the spot where the buck was standing and check for sign of a hit. In most cases there will be blood and/or hair. Then, look in the direction the buck ran. A deer that is hit in the lungs will spray bright blood off to the sides, and often pieces of lung will be hanging on brush. This deer will be found in short order. A buck hit in the heart will probably go farther and may not bleed for the first 40 or 50 yards. I recall one buck that I shot through the heart that kicked its hind legs out behind it and ran off before it disappeared over the edge of a ravine. I was incredulous when I could not find blood, but I stayed with the track and after it started running downhill I found a large blood clot. Looking ahead, I could see the buck lying dead on its side in the bottom of the ravine, with a steady blood trail between the clot and where it fell. A change in angle of the death run for a heart-shot buck — either uphill or downhill, or to leap over a fallen tree — will usually get the blood flowing.

Carry toilet paper or surveyor ribbon with you to mark a confusing or minimal blood trail. Often when you cannot find the next spot of blood, simply eyeballing the trail of toilet paper or ribbon will put you in line for the next spot. Of the two, I prefer toilet paper because it will break down and disappear within a few days. If you must use surveyor ribbon, return and pick up the ribbon once you are finished with the trail. It is, after all, litter at this point.

As long as you have a trail to follow, you must stay with it, even if the bleeding stops and all you are following is an uneven track that indicates the animal is limping. Of course this is a part of the respect we all should have for the white-tailed buck, but it also makes sense. Your odds of killing a wounded buck, or finding one that is fatally hit but not leaving a good trail to follow, are better than finding another large buck to shoot.

Several years ago my deer camp was making a drive, and one of the younger hunters hit a large buck as it ran for a thick swamp. Once the drive ended, two of us took the trail, which was nothing more than steady, dark drops on the dry, brown forest floor. As my friend Roger LaPenter (an expert tracker and former elk guide) looked for the next drop, I stood in place at the last drop — our hopes were not high for finding the animal. At one point Roger was slowly working his way down a logging road when I looked into a hole in the brush and spotted a drop of blood about eight feet away. The buck had veered off the trail and into the swamp. I called to Roger, and he crawled in on his hands and knees, and within minutes whistled to me because he'd found the 10-pointer.

The buck had been shot clear through from one side to the other, almost perfectly in the middle of its body. I gutted the deer before dragging it from the hellhole into which it had run, and could not figure out why the deer had died. Its lungs, heart, liver and paunch were all intact, but it had a hole in its diaphragm. The buck hadn't bled much and its body cavity was not filled with blood, either, yet there it lay. You must stay with a track as long as you can.

As you are tracking, pay attention to the natural world around you. Many times, a ruckus of coyotes or ravens may indicate that they have found your deer for you. Mark your last spot in the trail immediately to come back if need be, and follow the scavengers' call because there is a good chance your buck will be there.

GETTING THEM OUT

Because of the nature of the northwoods, hunters hoping to shoot a big whitetail need to anticipate a long drag. Earlier in this book I mentioned a 2-mile drag on dry ground with a giant buck, with two of us doing the pulling. It was the exuberance of youth that led me to hunt the spot and the naivete of youth that caused me to have no plan for getting such a buck out of the woods. To this day, I remain proud of the fact we got this animal out on the same day it was shot, but I do not plan to do that again.

None of us is getting any younger, and for the sake of hunting another day we should try to make a deer drag as easy as possible. Nothing beats a short drag to a truck or an ATV, but depending on where one hunts this may not be possible or even legal.

A child's plastic sled, or a commercially-made roll-up sled designed for dragging deer, can be helpful even on dry ground. On snow, there is almost nothing better.

You may wish to invest in a wheeled hand cart. Several models of varying sizes and prices are readily available through catalogs and stores that sell hunting equipment. On relatively flat ground and/or on trails, they can be a godsend, but they can be almost more hassle than they are worth in hilly country — a heavy deer strapped to a wheeled cart is hard to stop when going downhill.

If there are two or more hunters, use multiple drag ropes and drag in single file, with the draggers straddling the ropes. The lead dragger has the longest rope and because he is farther from the deer, the rope will be at a low angle. The second dragger uses a slightly shorter rope, and straddles the lead dragger's rope. The third guy uses a shorter rope than the second guy, and straddles the second rope. In brushy country with multiple draggers, this is almost too easy. Three or four guys in line can make very quick work of even a 200-pound-plus buck.

However, if you are hunting by yourself and you bag a buck where you cannot get it out in one day, consider hanging it from a tree and coming back to it the next day — with a sled or a cart, or friends, if you can find them. My camp members have done this countless times. Hang the buck head-up and coyotes and ravens will leave it alone for days. Only once has a member of our deer camp lost a buck in this manner, and this was to a late-wandering bear that had not yet taken to its

If their use is legal where one is hunting, nothing beats an ATV for getting a large buck out of a nasty spot.

den. Raise the buck high enough so its hindquarters are off the ground. This way the carcass can drain and cool overnight.

Throw the end of the drag rope over a branch that is high enough to get the buck off the ground, then lift the animal while at the same time holding the end of the rope in your hand. As you lift the deer, take slack out of the rope. At some point you will have to bear hug the buck and lift with your legs, but almost anyone can do this. Once the haunches are off the ground, tie off the rope and come back in the morning.

Modern equipment can be a terrific aid to the north-woods hunter. Kevin Schmidt and the author had numerous trail camera photos of this fine 8-pointer.

The Equipment Equation

O nly once has a buying decision that I have made been almost completely influenced by advertising, and it happened to concern my deer rifle. The full-color ad appeared in an outdoor magazine I was reading and showed the dramatic closeup of a snow-covered pump-action rifle held by two hands as if it was about to be fired. Snow swirled in the background. The ad proclaimed, "The rifles preferred for some very miserable reasons."

The idea was that the rifles being advertised would be reliable for their owner in any condition. Well, I happened to be in the market for a fast-handling deer rifle at the time, and really liked a pump-action shotgun that I owned that was made by the same manufacturer. I was sold.

Today, that rifle is like an extension of me. No matter how I am holding it, when I decide to shoot my fingers instantly find the safety and the buttstock always comes up to the right place on my shoulder. My cheek hits the stock and my right eye is instantly aligned with the crosshairs of the scope. Whether I am shooting from a tree stand at a relaxed buck or I am making a drive and the buck is starting to hit high gear in front of me, the entire action of shouldering the rifle, aiming and firing is fluid and natural. Everyone's deer rifle should fit them so perfectly.

Any discussion of hunting equipment has to start with the deer rifle, because that is the tool that makes the connection between the hunter and hunted.

THE RIFLE

As stated, you want your rifle to become an extension of yourself. It must fit your frame, be accurate and reliable. The style of rifle you choose should fit your style of hunting. If you primarily hunt from stands, a bolt-action rifle should be your choice because the action is usually the most accurate. However, if you are hunting afoot you will want a rifle that shoots multiple shots quickly, usually a semi-automatic or a pump. Of the two, a pump-action is considered the most reliable because semi-autos can be finicky when not cleaned properly.

Almost any centerfire cartridge is sufficient to bring down a big buck because bullet placement is far more important than firepower. I prefer a bigger cartridge simply because a 3½-year-old or older northwoods buck is a pretty big animal. And, sometimes, trees and branches get in the way of your shot. Ballistics tests conducted by gun writers have proven there is no such thing as a "brush-buster" caliber, but a big bullet pushed by a lot of powder has a better chance of getting through than a smaller caliber. I have seen enough deer that were killed by bullets that smashed through a tree before hitting hair to believe otherwise.

Another consideration in the bullet weight you choose is how it shoots through your rifle. I've tried several different bullet/weight combinations in my rifle that ranged from super-accurate to awful. For the record, my rifle is a .30-06, and I shoot premium grade 180-grain bullets through it.

Not everyone wants a telescopic sight on their rifle but I could not be without one. Rather than having to line up a front sight with a rear sight, I merely put the crosshairs where I want to shoot and squeeze the trigger. Plus, the magnification and light-gathering qualities give the shooter a better view of his target, so he is going to shoot more accurately. Long-range shots are a rarity in the northwoods, so conventional fixed-power or variable-power scopes are sufficient. A stand-hunter may prefer a 3x9-power, but since I am on the move a lot when making drives, I use a 2x7-power scope. When I am hunting afoot I dial the scope down to 2-power, and when I am on stand I keep it on 3- or 3½-power, but the higher magnification is there should I need it for a more difficult shot. If you leave your scope set on a higher power you may not have a sufficient field of view to quickly find your target through the scope.

If you are considering a scope purchase, do yourself a favor and buy the best you can afford. I have had the same deer rifle for over 30 years, but it has been paired with three scopes in that time. The first two were low-end models that had a litany of issues before their accuracy faded away; the third is simply remarkable but cost twice as much as the first two. The first year I hunted with the high quality scope I tripped and fell on it while trying to get in position to shoot at a running deer, yet when I checked it on the shooting range the next day its point of impact had not changed at all. I was surprised yet pleased, because similar incidents had knocked both of the first two scopes out of alignment at one time or another. Had I just purchased the better scope in the first place I would have had fewer problems and spent less money in total.

Your rifle should have some kind of adjustable sling. There are few things worse than trying to drag a buck out of the woods while also carrying your rifle in one hand. When hunting with others, if you sling your rifle over your shoulder, the barrel will be pointed upward and in a safe direction. If snow or mud makes walking treacherous, as when climbing or descending a hill, unload your rifle and sling it so you can use both hands to try to keep yourself upright.

I place a piece of black tape over the end of my barrel while hunting to keep it from being plugged with snow or mud. Wrap additional tape around the barrel in case you shoot and need to replace the original tape.

OTHER ESSENTIALS

When I hunt deer, I carry the following essential equipment: a belt knife with a fixed, 4-inch blade; a quality compass; a 10-foot length of ¼-inch nylon rope; an extra magazine loaded with shells; a cellphone; toilet paper; a bottle of water; a sandwich; and bite-size candy bars.

If I'm going to make drives that day or am uncertain of locating my stand location in the pre-dawn darkness, I carry a hand-held GPS. I do not hunt in areas where an overnight stay may be required, but for those who do, a space-blanket and waterproof matches or a lighter would be important.

When hunting alone, I carry a waterproof point-and-shoot digital camera and a small tripod. Buck photos are always better if taken where the animal dropped, rather than back at camp or in the back of a pick-up truck.

If I am hunting with someone else who could take photos should I get a buck, I rely on my cellphone and leave both the camera and tripod back in camp. High-end phones with a camera application can take remarkable images; in fact, some of the photos in this book were taken with my cellphone. The phone can also be a lifesaver to call for help if you were to fall from a tree stand and are dangling from your safety harness.

When the air temperatures are really cold, it helps to place heat packs in your mittens, over your chest and the small of your back, and even in your boots.

I also carry a gallon-size, zip-top plastic bag to carry a buck's tenderloins. The tenderloins are a strip of meat along each side of the spine on the inside of the body cavity, which I fillet out after gutting a buck. These cuts of venison dry very quickly and if you wait until you hang the buck back at camp later that evening, or if you forget about it until the next day, they will not be as good as if you take them out of the body cavity immediately. If there is snow on the ground, set them in the snow to cool while you clean your knife and get the deer and your equipment ready to begin dragging.

THE WELL-ATTIRED HUNTER

Dressing properly for stand-hunting is hugely different from dressing correctly for still-hunting, tracking, or driving, from the top of your head to your feet. There are two constants — always go with wool or fleece instead of cotton, and high-tech long underwear really is worth the price.

Wool and fleece, and cotton, are similar in that they're quiet fabrics that are unlikely to spook deer. However, wool and fleece remain warm when wet, whereas cotton will not. A wet hunter wearing cotton will be a cold hunter, who might as well come out of the woods because he will never warm up completely.

I have already discussed the remainder of my hunting attire while stand-hunting or when on the move in previous chapters, so there is no need to repeat it here.

I prefer a blaze orange vest rather than a parka because of the versatility it affords. On the first day of the hunt, I can affix my backtag to it (if required by law) and put the essentials in the pockets, and then wear it without changing anything, regardless if I am in a stand or on the move. I just pull it over my other clothing and I am ready to hunt.

My footwear varies according to how I plan to hunt for the day, too. I used to wear pac-style boots, with leather tops and rubber bottoms, but I switched when I found the high-tech stuff to be so much lighter and warmer. When bow-hunting, I wear knee-high rubber boots with 800 grams of Thinsulate.

For bow-hunting, let's just say I have lots of camouflage clothing of varying weights and insulation. Wisconsin's bow season runs from the middle of September until early January, and the air temperature can vary by more than a hundred degrees — from highs in the 80s to lows in the minus-20s during that period. Now, I prefer not to hunt with a bow when the air temperature is more than 65 degrees or colder than 10, but that is still a huge range. I always wear scent-containing clothing and, if it is cold, I dress in layers without bulking up too badly.

The author pauses at the conclusion of a drive on a cold, snowy day. The clothes he wears while hunting vary with the day's plans and weather. A fast-shooting rifle is essential.

SCENT-CONTAINING CLOTHING

One of the most beneficial purchases I have made of deer hunting equipment is scent-containing clothing — I have always been one to keep my clothing and myself as scent-free as possible, and to hunt only from stands located in a favorable wind. I had been skeptical about the advertising promises made for scent-containing clothing, but decided to try it. The fact that I began seeing bigger bucks immediately could be coincidental, but likely not. Something else I began seeing was deer bedding within yards of my stand and, in some cases, downwind or beneath it!

You can make scent-containing clothing as elaborate as you want. With some hunters, every layer they wear contains a scent inhibitor. I typically wear one layer of such scent-containing clothing from head to toe — headcover, jacket or shirt, and pants. If I hope to fool deer that are extremely close, as when bow-hunting, I wear knee-high rubber boots with the pants legs tucked in.

If you want to prove the value of scent-containing clothing in an inexpensive manner, spend twenty-five dollars and buy a headcover. Wear it in your stand and, when you are ready to leave, take a big whiff of the inside of the headcover as you pull it off — you should get a real strong idea of the odor given off by your hair and the top of your head, even if you had bathed in scent-free soap.

I still play the wind, and keep myself and my clothing as scent-free as possible (using both body and clothing soaps that eliminate scent). I never wear my hunting clothing for anything else, and during the off-season I store it in air-tight plastic bins.

If such clothing has one downside, it does not breathe well. Therefore, I will not wear it on the move. I wear scent-containing clothing only while hunting from a stand.

TRAIL CAMERAS YIELD ESSENTIAL INTEL

One piece of high-tech equipment that can really help your hunting is a trail camera. I prefer infrared models, even though some argue they spook deer, and their night photo quality is not as good as flash cameras. ("Black flash" infrared cameras are the latest generation at this writing, and from my initial experience with them they seem to not bother deer at all.) Infrared models simply use less battery power to operate; there are few things more disappointing than going to your stand and finding the "low battery" light glowing. It likely will not matter at all to your hunt that day, but the felt disappointment is very real.

Trail cameras will give you an idea of the size of bucks in the area. If after several weeks of use they do not reveal a buck of the quality that you want, the camera just saved you a bunch of time because you now know you do not need to hunt that stand. Be careful, however, as to when you make such judgment about a stand. Everything changes with the rut, and a camera overlooking a stand that is taking pictures of only small bucks and does can suddenly capture images of big bucks moving through once the rut starts. Does are the key to a stand that didn't initially appear promising.

Cameras can also reveal if a particular buck is on a schedule. If he only visits your stand in the afternoon, you can consider hunting elsewhere in the morning.

Trail cameras can also be frustrating by picturing bucks that remain nocturnal. Often, that is just the nature of a big buck, but you can use the "intelligence" in a positive manner by searching out a new stand site that is closer to where you think the buck is bedding, increasing the likelihood of seeing it on its feet during legal shooting time. Even if a buck only shows up at night, just knowing he is in the area is an incentive to hunt that stand because they do make mistakes.

A couple of tips:

• A big buck's back is only as high as the waist of an average-sized man, so if you set your cameras waist-high your photos should be framed correctly.

• I like to set and check my cameras on rainy days, which will wash away any scent I may leave. If you must tend to the camera on a dry day, use a scent-eliminating spray on the camera and anything else you may have touched.

• Trail cameras typically allow for multiple resolution settings. Set at their highest resolution, they will allow you to enlarge images to study a buck's antlers, or allow for a nice printed enlargement should you choose to do so.

• I like to set my cameras for a 2-minute delay between photos. I do not need every photo of every deer in the area; I only want to know what deer are there.

• You do not need to purchase a memory card "viewer." Most trail cameras save photos as .jpg files to a secure digital (SD) card, and most point-and-shoot automatic cameras use the same kind of card to take the same format photo file. Just take the card out of your trail camera and put it in your automatic camera and you will be able to review your photos.

• Trail cameras often work better with higher-quality batteries.

• A cable lock is a cheap way of guaranteeing your camera will still be there when you come back to check it. Bears often lick, bite, and sometimes destroy cameras, so a protective "bear box," may be a wise investment if you're setting cameras before

One of many trail camera photos of the 8-point buck pictured at the outset of this chapter. Its large body size made its antlers seem smaller than they really were.

Stealth Cam   10/15/2011   20:49:36   ●   30F

Modern technology can help the northwoods hunter. Here, a 9-pointer was captured by a trail camera as it walked through the shooting lane of one of the author's stands during daylight hours. The author told a friend to hunt there the next day, and the friend killed a different buck from this stand.

they den up. (The last photo a friend's trail camera ever took was of the inside of a bear's mouth!) I no longer buy bear boxes because trail camera size and shape seem to change annually. Since the boxes are usually model-specific they quickly become obsolete.

Muzzleloading rifles are as accurate as any centerfire rifle. The author had a narrow window to make the shot on this 200-pound 11-pointer.

THE MUZZLELOADING ALTERNATIVE

I will never forget the Hawken carbine I used in Wisconsin's first modern day muzzleloader season in 1991. The rifle fired when an external hammer slammed onto a cap and ignited honest-to-goodness black powder that belched an all-lead bullet through an octagonal barrel. Before the season, I practiced with various amounts of powder to find a charge my rifle preferred, and with plenty of practice I eventually felt lethal to deer out to a range of about 75 yards. Because it was black powder, every shot demanded an extensive cleaning of the barrel, so the commitment was considerable.

That first season was open for antlerless deer only, and the weather was extremely cold. Still, I hunted hard, and when a large doe rose up from its bed on a south-facing hillside I took my time to aim but was disappointed when my gun failed to fire. The extremes in temperature had caused moisture build-up in the barrel which dampened the charge — as well as my first muzzleloader hunt.

Compare that to the muzzleloading rifle I use today. Rather than carefully-measured powder, I simply drop three 50-grain pellets into the barrel and ram a ballistic-tipped bullet down until it is tight. The charge is set off when an internal, in-line firing pin ignites a 209 shotgun primer. This rifle sports a sling, a camouflage synthetic stock, a stainless steel barrel and action, and is topped with a 3x9-power scope, and when it needs cleaning the effort required is almost an afterthought.

Both muzzleloader types — traditional and modern — are legal to use in most locales nowadays despite their only similarity being that they are loaded from the barrel. While some who use traditional muzzleloaders would prefer that you do, too, I am not going to further that debate. Use whatever rifle you want and go as minimal or modern as you want. This chapter is included in this book to explain how anybody who wants to hunt more can easily become proficient with a muzzleloading rifle.

After that first season with the Hawken, I did not use a muzzleloader again for nearly a decade. The lure of more days in the woods drew me back and I bought a modern in-line. The first day in the woods with the new muzzleloader was a revelation — it seemed so much like bow-hunting because the woods were quiet and the deer moved about on their own, yet I had a rifle across my lap. The first deer I killed with it was a spike buck that made the mistake of wandering too close to a guy who was eager to find out what it was like to shoot a muzzleloader at a deer. He was the smallest buck I have ever taken, yet one I will always remember.

Going Modern

Since I have taken the modern muzzleloader route, I have failed only once (at this writing) to kill a deer that I wanted to take home. My muzzleloader was topped with a 1-power scope because Wisconsin law at the time required open sites or a non-magnifying scope. The doe was the first deer that I had ever viewed through such a scope and I was stunned when the animal appeared to be smaller than real-life. My head snapped up and I blinked, then looked through the scope, blinked again, and raised my head again. I know that when the rifle fired my cheek was not pressed to the stock, and the result was a clean miss at 40 yards.

Now my muzzleloader carries a conventional magnifying scope and its accuracy out to 100 yards is as good as that of a fine rifle. Consider the largest buck I have killed with a muzzleloader as of this writing, the 11-pointer discussed in the "Deer Calls & Common Scents" chapter. We had trail camera photos of this animal that clearly showed a distinctive rack, and I knew exactly which deer it was as soon as its head entered the shooting lane 35 yards away. The problem was the buck stopped and did not step into the shooting lane; only its neck and head were visible, and his body from the base of his neck back was obscured by trees. The buck just stood there, looking one way and then the other for the intruding buck it thought it had heard.

After an agonizing wait I finally decided to aim where the base of the buck's skull met its neck. I felt confident that I could make the shot because I had the rifle supported with a shooting stick, and I had just drilled a perfect bull's-eye at 50 yards a couple days earlier on the rifle range. The crosshairs settled, the muzzy barked, and when the smoke cleared the big buck lay on its side with a half-inch hole in its neck — precisely where I had aimed.

Rigging Up

You can buy a kit and build your own Hawken, carry your powder in a home-made powder horn, wear fringed buckskin, and urinate down your barrel to clean it. Or, you can step into the nearest box store and plunk down anywhere from $150 to $1,000 and walk out with everything you need to get started. Regardless of the route you choose, your rifle will be highly effective on deer, will be remarkably accurate, and will give you the opportunity to extend your deer hunting season each year.

The easiest route to getting started in muzzleloading is simplicity. You can buy a beginner's kit from any box store, but the shopping list is not long. Here is what you need:

• Rifle — Anything larger than a rifled .40-caliber is legal for hunting deer in many locations, but the .50-caliber is what most hunters choose because of a near-perfect combination of ballistics and knock-down power. Break actions are replacing bolt-actions because they are easier to prime and clean. The rifle will come with a ramrod that fits beneath the barrel. The ramrod is used for seating the bullet as well as cleaning the rifle.

• Propellent — This launches the bullet. Many hunters simply choose pelletized black powder substitutes because they are easier to use and some leave much less fouling in your rifle barrel than others. You will need two or three 50-grain pellets (a total of 100 or 150 grains) for each charge. Before you use 150 grains, make sure your rifle is capable of shooting it because some are not.

• Primers — The primer will be struck by your rifle's firing pin or hammer and ignites the propellant. 209 shotgun primers work great, but special muzzleloader primers do not burn as hot and thus leave less residue in the barrel. This makes for easier cleaning.

• Bullets — The alloy, saboted, ballistic-tipped bullets I use could not be any easier. I slip three powder pellets down the barrel and push the bullet firmly on top of the charge. Put a primer in the breach and the gun is ready to shoot. I shoot a 295-grain bullet.

• Bullet starter — This handy tool allows you to get the bullet started in the muzzle of the barrel. After it is pushed a few inches down you finish the job with the ramrod. A tip — once the bullet is firmly seated atop the charge (propellant), score the ramrod evenly with the top of the barrel. Now you have a handy reference to check your bullet's seating every time you load, because a gap between the powder and bullet may create pressure as the powder ignites that could damage your barrel. At the very least it may cause an inaccurate shot.

• Cleaning kit — This will include solvent, patches, a wire brush for the breach, and some kind of lubricant/rust inhibitor. You will also need a brass brush that matches your muzzy's caliber to clean the barrel. You do not want to skimp here — a clean gun always fires, whereas a dirty gun may be gummed up beyond use. A dirty barrel can negatively affect accuracy.

• Other items — If you buy a bolt-action muzzleloader, you will find that a tool for inserting the 209 primers is invaluable. A speed-loader provides a waterproof way to carry extra charges (bullets, pellets and primers). I still carry one, but I have found that it is just as easy to dump the charges onto the ground as load the rifle when I am excited, because the clear plastic tubes of the speed-loader do not fit inside the muzzle of the rifle. A "possibles bag" is essentially a man-purse that provides a handy way to carry tools, charges and cleaning supplies. A small safety pin helps clear the fire hole of a breach plug. Finally, I usually carry a shooting stick because it helps ensure that my single shot will count.

Regardless if you use iron sights or a scope, sight your muzzleloader like any other rifle.

That's it! With minimal effort these special rifles can put you in the woods for what some consider the most enjoyable days of the year.

A much-younger version of the author contemplates the events that led to the killing of the "Thanksgiving Buck."

Deer Tales: The Thanksgiving Buck

The following incident occurred during Wisconsin's 1992 gun season and involves a deer that became known in the pages of my hunting camp's logbook as the "Thanksgiving Buck." Both Wisconsin Outdoor Journal *and* Wisconsin Outdoor News *magazines have carried versions of this story in their pages. The surreal events of this hunt haunt me to this day.*

Paul Bietka looked up from the tracking job before him. His expression was serious, and there was not a hint of optimism about him. "What do you want to do?" he asked.

"I can't give up, Paul," I replied. "I've got to find this deer."

"I knew you were going to say that. But it's getting dark, and we've got to get across the river. You can come back for him in the morning," Paul reasoned. "With any luck, he'll bed down as soon as we get off his track, and then you can jump him up and get him tomorrow."

Paul was making sense. Darkness was rapidly approaching, and the buck had not given any indication it was going to die soon. Its track had taken us through a popple stand and into some pines, where little snow on the ground made for tough tracking. And the blood trail, which at one time had been so promising, was becoming sparse. We had been due at the river crossing an hour earlier, but we were sure the other members of our hunting group had heard my gunshots and were willing to accept our tardiness.

Realizing my thinking was clouded by the disappointment of having to leave a wounded buck in the woods overnight, I gave in to Paul's logic and walked down the hill to the river with him.

I had been still-hunting along the edge of a steep ravine where a tiny stream had spent eons cutting through the red clay soil on its way to another creek before dumping into the river. It had been a good day to be alone in the deer woods of Wisconsin. I had seen a doe that morning and had watched a fisher hunt along a creek. I was pleased with my day as I headed toward the river crossing and the 3 o'clock rendezvous time.

The buck spotted me the instant I saw him. He was one-third of the way up the far side of the ravine I had been sneaking along. He snorted and bolted, running to the left and uphill. I swung my pump-action rifle with the deer, found it in the scope, led him by a nose, and squeezed off a shot. The buck's back legs buckled, but he caught himself, and I sent another round on its way when the crosshairs found their place ahead of the running deer's chest. Through the scope, I watched the buck stagger and vanish amidst the popples.

Certain the deer was down, I crossed the ravine and searched for sign of a hit. I discovered where a slug from my .30-06 had plowed into the soil, showering the scattered snow patches with small bits of dirt. And then I found the first sign of a wounded deer — several drops of bright blood spattered onto the snow and up the buck's trail. I found a place where bright-colored blood had spurted out. A puddle of the bright blood stained the snow where the buck had stepped over a log.

The sign was looking good.

That's when Paul showed up. On his way to the river crossing he heard my shots and came over to investigate. "Nice buck," I told Paul. "I'm certain he's just up the trail."

But as my wristwatch neared 4 p.m. we still hadn't found the buck. He had led us through a confusing tangle of small popples, the blood trail diminishing to a fleck in the snow here, a drop there. Then it took us into a stand of tall pines where very little snow remained. We tracked the buck by finding places where its hooves had disturbed pine needles, and felt like we had made a major find when we discovered two downed trees, both lying about a foot and half off the ground, that the buck had dragged itself across. Snow on the tree trunks had been brushed off, and blood was smeared on the snow and bark. "He should have been able to bound, or at least step, over these logs without any problem," Paul noted. "I think he's hit farther back than you thought."

I described the sight picture to Paul then, being careful to mention that I had led the running buck in the scope. In my mind's eye I could still see the buck moving up the hill, my scope's crosshairs just ahead of the heart/lung area. And I had continued to swing the rifle with the running deer, just as I had done on other running deer I'd killed in previous years. The bullet should have short-circuited the buck in a matter of minutes, if that long. I was certain of the shot — otherwise I wouldn't have taken it. And I had seen the buck's back legs buckle, hadn't I?

"You must have had a deflection," Paul surmised. "There must have been something between you and the buck that knocked your bullet out of whack."

That's fine, I thought. I've got an excuse why the buck isn't already dead and tagged. But that's little consolation when you're leaving the woods for the night and there's a wounded deer out there that's your responsibility.

Alone in the deer shack that night, I had plenty of time to think about the task that lay before me. With the next day being Thanksgiving, most of the gang had left the woods to get "civilized," including Paul. I had unfinished business left in the woods, so I stayed behind. Another member of our hunting crew, Paul Ratliff, would be out to the shack in the morning to help me trail the buck.

After a quick dinner of venison tenderloin from one of the other deer bagged by the crew, I sat and read through the pages of the camp log. This camp's origins date back to around World War II, and the log's pages are a colorful piece of Wisconsin deer hunting history. Occasionally, I found reference to someone wounding a deer; more often than not the deer was killed the next day. That's the way it should be with wounded deer. But every so often there was mention of one that wasn't killed.

The camp log told me that hunters before me and hunters after me will occasionally not be able to track down a wounded deer. It's an unfortunate, but inevitable, occurrence that some deer will not die quickly at the hands of hunters. No matter how much a hunter practices with his rifle in preparation for the season, there's little that can be done about the unseen twig or branch that sometimes deflects a bullet. What the camp log didn't tell me was how to track down the deer I'd hit, or how to cope with the personal disappointment of a non-clean kill. This, I figured, I would have to learn for myself.

I closed the cover of the camp log and reminisced about other deer I had taken over the years. All had been quick, humane kills, requiring little tracking, if any. Several, in fact, had dropped on the spot. Still, there was that forkhorn some years before. Unbeknownst to me, my scope had been knocked out of alignment, probably when I bumped it the night before. It wasn't jarred that badly, I thought, but apparently it was enough to throw the point of aim well off. The forkie offered me a standing 25-yard shot, but my slug grazed his brisket instead of puncturing his lungs. That little buck took me on a tour of the deer woods for four miles before the bleeding had completely stopped and his track became lost in a maze of other fresh deer tracks. That buck was strong and moving well when I left him, and I am positive the wound was superficial and he survived. Still, it took me years to get over the fact that I'd left a wounded deer in the woods.

The buck this story is about, however, was hurt much worse than that forkhorn. He wouldn't survive, and would probably end up as coyote feed if I didn't get him. I knew that all too well, and thinking about it left a bitter taste in my mouth. I stepped onto the back porch of the deer shack and listened to the wind in the pines. I thought about the buck and wondered what it was doing, then said a quick prayer for help and vowed that I wouldn't give up on the track.

Early the next morning Paul Ratliff and I crossed the river and started climbing the hill. Halfway to the top a deer burst from its bed and ran off through the cedars.

"Buck!" Paul hissed. "A nice one!"

Our rifles barked and the buck stopped. I remember the sight through my scope as being like a picture in a magazine — a beautiful buck looking back at us through the cedars. I could see the entire front half of the deer, so I settled the crosshairs behind his shoulder and squeezed the trigger. My rifle spoke and the deer disappeared.

The buck lay in the snow and breathed its last as we approached. First we admired the wide, 8-point rack, and then Paul and I turned and gave each other a high-five. "I couldn't believe that he just stopped and gave you such an easy shot,"

Paul said. "Usually, when you jump a buck they don't wait around to see what happens next."

Then we saw it — the buck's right rear leg was broken and dangling, a grotesque wound that was out of place on such a handsome animal. "One of our first shots must have hit him and that's why he didn't keep running," Paul figured.

I bent over to tag the buck, and then paused. "Whose tag should we put on him?" I asked.

"You killed it. It's your deer so put your tag on it," Paul stated.

"But I've still got that deer that I hit yesterday."

"That deer isn't dead yet. I've still got my tag, so if we catch up to him I'll tag it."

I cut the appropriate slits on the tag and tied it to the buck's antlers. I then field dressed it, taking care to fillet out the tenderloins for a camp meal. We placed the deer where it could drain, then proceeded up the hill to take the track of the wounded buck — though we were pleased with the nice buck I had just killed, we both realized our job was far from finished.

The track wasn't hard to locate once we reached the top of the hill. We found it immediately, well beyond where Paul Bietka and I had left it the day before. Because of a lack of snow, the track was getting hard to follow when we quit for the day Wednesday. Where Paul Ratliff and I picked up the trail Thursday, the deer had walked where a good blanket of snow remained. Still, the blood trail was little more than a speck of blood every 30 feet or so. Paul, being a better tracker than me, followed the slots while I circled to the side, keeping my eyes on the woods in front of us.

"Stevie ... this deer is definitely hit in the right rear leg," Paul called to me. "He stood here for a while, probably listening to you two tracking him, and there's seven or eight drops of blood in the snow at his right rear leg."

"Paul ... the buck I just shot was hit in the right rear leg. Do you think ..."

"Might be. I'll stay on the track and you backtrack that buck and find out."

I returned to the downed buck and examined the leg wound. Blood had matted the hair down to the hoof, something that wouldn't have happened if the buck had been hit in the leg just moments before I shot it through the chest. Encouraged, I backtracked the buck to where it had been bedded among the skeletons of some long-dead cedars.

From 10 feet away I had my answer. The bed was easy to find — a brown spot on the white-frosted hillside. A couple of red splotches on the dead, brown cedar leaves looked like blood, and I quickly knelt down and grabbed an individual leaf. The blood smeared between my fingers — it was the same buck I had wounded the day before!

A variety of emotions welled up inside of me and I slumped against a cedar trunk, the cedar leaf still in my hand. I stared at the buck's bed and wondered what thoughts had gone through its head the night before as it lay on the hillside, overlooking the river. The location of where the buck bedded — so close to a spot where our camp members have climbed the hill out of the river bottom for decades — still makes me shudder. Did the buck choose his bed knowing that he wouldn't make it through the coming winter, and that we'd be back the next day? Was he, in fact, waiting for us? This would suggest deer are conscious of their own mortality. Thoughts such as this would be quickly dismissed by science ... yet they remain with me to this day because I lived the events recorded on these pages.

After collecting my own thoughts for a few moments, I walked back up the hill to get Paul and tell him the news.

Later, as I showed Paul the blood in the bed, he admitted he didn't think we would get the deer as we followed its track.

"Neither did I," I confessed. "But I couldn't give up on the track."

"I knew you wouldn't," Paul smiled. "Now let's get him back to camp."

It was Thanksgiving, and dinner awaited. But that year I knew it would be a special holiday for I had yet another reason to give thanks.

DEER CAMP

A renaissance of sorts has occurred in the world of the traditional deer camp. It was not long ago when some predicted the end of deer camps, blaming mobile hunters who were too busy for extended hunts. Though I have no way of proving it, my guess is that deer camps are back. Maybe you won't find a big crew leaving civilization on Friday and emerging from the woods bewhiskered and smelly a week and a half later, but hunters are banding together again because, let's face it, deer camps are fun.

Deer camp allows the modern hunter to escape work and worries for as long as his vacation time and obligations allow. While it's not for everyone, many find joy in hunting together, or at least joining together at night to share stories and success. The banter and humor are, at best, sophomoric, but nobody cares. Deer camp members may not have seen each other since they closed camp the previous fall, but when the rutting moon rises they feel their camp's call. They may get more fresh air, walk more miles, eat more food and snore more loudly than any other time of year, and they wouldn't have it any other way.

For this look at deer camps, I've drawn some of the better excerpts from the log of my own hunting camp, the Barking Spider Lodge, as well as from the log of a northern Wisconsin camp from the early 1900s. For my camp, I chronicled the passages in relative order, while I summarized the voluminous reports of the Man-I-Do-Wish Hunting Camp.

THE BARKING SPIDER LODGE

FRIDAY, NOVEMBER 18, 2005

Paul, Joe, Russ, Eric, Steve and Brant came out early to ready the shack. We strung the boat across the river. Brant and Steve found the former's tree stand crushed when its tree was blown over.

While looking for something in the old shack, Eric encountered an angry porcupine beneath an old mattress, so the crew sent Brant to "get the old mattress from the old shack." As all hands watched, Brant disappeared into the old shack only to soon come running out with a look of fear in his eyes. Mad porkies will do that to you.

Darrel and Ryan came out later. Dinner was Steve's Deer Butt Chili. Poker entertained all.

SATURDAY, NOVEMBER 23, 1996, OPENING DAY

Eric, Ryan, Aaron, Tom, Ben, Matt, Russ, Steve, Darrel and Garth crossed the river. Paul and Babs hunted the cabin side. Crossing the river was difficult as it was half-frozen so every deer this side of the Mason Dixon Line knew we were coming. Shelf ice covered all the lower trails and we had to bust through it to get up the hill.

The first shot was fired by Aaron in a tree stand. He had his first run-in with the Bullet-Proof Doe, and saw three others with it. Matt, Eric and Ryan saw deer but no shots. We were all back at the Spike Camp eating lunch when we heard three shots. Fifteen minutes later, Aaron came running back. He had shot an 11-point buck from his stand, his first deer. Congratulations Aaron. He was so excited he jumped in the creek and got all wet. Garth shot a nice doe, his first deer. Congratulations Garth. Paul shot a small deer out by the farm in the pines. Tenderloins were enjoyed that night. A good hunt.

Saturday, November 17, 2007, Opening Day

Low 30s, snow on and off all day, one inch of accumulation. Eric, Tom, Darrel and Brant crossed the river. Paul, Roger, Russ, Steve and Joe hunted north. Busy time in the morning. Steve shot a 6-pointer at 7:50, Brant shot a spike at 8:15, Eric shot an 8-pointer at 8:30 and Roger shot a 10-pointer. Eric saw four deer total, Brant saw six. Joe passed up a spike, and Paul and Russ saw does and fawns. Eric named his buck "Elmo the Flying Deer." For explanation, ask him.

Dinner was tenderloins and fried spuds, and poker was played. Badgers 41, Gophers 34.

Sunday, November 18, 2001

Day 2 of "Tom Wishes He Got In The Buck Pool" dawned early as some of the crew rolled out early to see the Leonid Meteor Shower. The boys said it was as spectacular as the scientists predicted, and could only have been better had the meteors somehow ingested Russ' 16-Bean Soup. Maybe next year he can afford 17 beans.

Eric, Darrel, Russ, Ryan and Steve hunted south of the river. Paul R. and Babs, Paul B. and Jer, and Tom and his boys hunted north. Darrel missed a buck in the Pine Stump. Eric made friends with a fawn, and Paul R. missed a fawn.

Paul R. finished building the shower and Steve was the first to use it because he needed it badly.

Second day of 60-degree weather. Rain this afternoon and night. If it turns to snow as the weather guessers predict, we'll be a happy crew.

Sunday, November 20, 2005

Eric, Darrel, Russ, Steve, Ryan, Brant, Tom and his sons crossed the river. Joe and Paul stayed north. Steve shot a doe shortly after crossing the river and dropped it 85 paces from the boat. Brant missed a small buck from Steve's stand. Tommy C. saw a doe.

Back at camp, Joe saw a buck fawn in the ravine behind camp while getting spring water. Upon return to camp, Ryan saw the same deer. So Darrel poked and moseyed to the saddle and bagged the suicidal deer. Leave it to Darrel to pick on a poor, disadvantaged orphan.

36 degrees, no snow any more, very muddy.

MONDAY, NOVEMBER 25, 1996

Darrel, Garth, Russ, Roger and Steve tried to cross the river, but it froze the night before. We decided to let it harden and hunted the north side of the river.

We drove the hillside to Babs' stand. Steve jumped two but his gun tangled in the brush and he couldn't shoot. Then we drove to Eric's Park and Roger saw one. Then we made the drive to Roger's old stand.

Looking down the survey line, Roger spotted a Kahuna. Shouldering his popgun and holding a foot over its back, Rog learned a .44 mag is not a long-range weapon. Maybe had he run at the deer, the running start would have helped the slug ... then again, maybe not.

Nobody saw anything in the afternoon.

MONDAY, NOVEMBER 22, 1999

Rain greeted us and lasted until about 11. Not much moving. Paul B. saw two deer and Darrel saw four in the Ravine Drive. Eric, Roger and Steve saw a bear.

The last drive was from the end of the Popple Flats to the Pine Stump. Darrel pushed four deer past Eric — about four feet past Eric — and he shot a doe. Eric's doe is hanging near Elm Creek — we'll rent a helicopter to get it out. Good thing Ryan owes Eric about eight miles of deer dragging. Said Eric:

"I'd have been able to get all four if I had a baseball bat."

TUESDAY, NOVEMBER 20, 2007

Eric, Joe, Russ, Rob L., Darrel and Steve in camp and hunted north of the river until noon. The only deer seen was the Cheshire Doe, seen by Steve. We hunted on our own in the afternoon.

Dinner was organic Polish sausage and cheesy potatoes. In the evening poker game, a game of Gutshot Fawn ended with all hands having full-houses! Later, Eric won a hand with a pair of deuces, prompting Darrel to say, and I quote: "I'm twice the poker player he is!"

TUESDAY, NOVEMBER 21, 1995

A great day. The boys woke up to a fresh powder of snow and crossed the river. We didn't use Eric's 4-wheeler nor did we bump along in the boat as we were able to walk on the ice. The deer didn't know what hit them.

Paul R. and Steve drove the First Drive and Roger shot a big doe, and saw a buck and four other deer. Eric shot at the

Barking Spider Lodge

Bullet-Proof Doe but it escaped unscathed.

The next drive by Eric and Darrel pushed out three. Steve shot at the Bullet-Proof Doe, again to no avail. Paul R. shot a doe.

Roger and Paul R. then drove the second half of the First Drive. Steve, on stand, shot a spike buck as the animal walked over to see what all the ruckus was.

The boys met at the Spike Camp. Roger and Paul built a fire and got cozy while a doe and fawn sneaked up on them. Alert hunter Eric spotted the deer as they prepared to attack the Spike Camp and ran them off without firing a shot.

We then drove the Popple Flats. Roger and Darrel each dispatched suicidal does that ran right toward them.

Steve went back to the Rope for the pre-arranged Pine Stump drive and jumped a Big Kahuna bedded 30 yards away from the Rope. Even though it "disappeared" on the shot, the buck's tracks were later found. It "disappeared" because it was running so fast no human eye could follow.

We then drove behind the camp and Roger jumped three big does that deftly stayed just out of Darrel's field of fire.

Dinner was tenderloins and taters. Many lies were told and boasts were made. Five deer for the day.

WEDNESDAY, NOVEMBER 26, 1997

Eric, Ryan, Darrel, Steve, Aaron, Hugo and Joey R. showed up. Joey forgot his rifle. Everyone crossed the river except Joey. Ryan insisted he should trade stands with Aaron, and then Aaron shot a spike buck from Ryan's stand.

Eric saw a doe and spared its life.

Joey R. and Paul R. hunted north of the river. Joey had a deer nearby but he needs to eat fewer beans.

Three bucks in two years for Aaron. It sounds like the curse of ten years of does and fawns coming up.

WEDNESDAY, NOVEMBER 25, 2003

Day 3 of hunting in a Hallmark postcard. Merry Christmas. Steve shot a doe. Other does and fawns seen but no shots taken.

Eric made his special garlic parmesan alfredo for supper and we ate, then we ate some more. Overheard at the poker table: "Can I buy a dollar's worth of chips?"

FRIDAY, NOVEMBER 26, 2010

A bunch of turkeys head out after Thanksgiving. Eric, Ryan, Steve, Russ, Caleb F., Matt, Ben, Bruce, Josh and Noah crossed the river, but first our resident lumberjack and resident engineer had to chop a crossing through the ice. Photographic record was made in case of insurance necessities for the surviving widows.

Well, where to begin? Seven deer came out of the First Drive, all bald. One baldie seen in the ravine. Then we drove the Popple Flats and saw 12, including at least two bulletproof bucks. We also saw six wolves. Then we made the Pine Stump Drive but the wolves had already made it for us.

Steve saw a doe and fawn from his stand in the evening. That makes 22 deer seen by the camp members and none

Spike Camp

killed for the day.

At camp, dinner was Eric's Polish sausages and bean surprise, and Steve's venison brats. A musical night.

FRIDAY, NOVEMBER 25, 2011

A good day. Big crew out. Eric, Ryan, Matt, Steve, Russ, Noah, Josh, Mark S., Doug L., and Colin and Ian crossed the river. Lots of deer moving in the First Drive, and Josh missed a doe. (Joe, Colin and Ian had youth tags and could kill does.)

Nothing in the Tamarack and Ravine drives, and Eric saw a bear. We then drove the Popple Flats to the north with standers strung out in the Cabin Ravine. Steve was on the end of Pine Stump Point and went to "full automatic." When the smoke cleared and the woods were quiet again, a nice 8-point buck lay dead. Then Josh started shooting and killed two does, one really big. Colin shot twice at a spike but missed. We then dragged the deer out, crossing the mighty White River after dark.

Eric made whitefish alfredo for dinner, which was 100 times better than his pork/potato/rutabaga/sauerkraut surprise debacle of the other night.

SATURDAY, NOVEMBER 25, 2006

A day of near-misses and then a hit. Big crew — Eric, Ryan, Darrel, Russ, Steve, Brant, Tom, Ben and Tommy crossed the river. Bruce and Noah, too, crossed the river, fortified by Bruce's egg croissants.

Bruce proceeded to miss a doe in the First Drive. In the Ravine, Steve jumped a doe but couldn't get a decent shot. Then a buck and several does ran up behind Eric in the Ravine to within 30 feet but escaped unscathed into the Popple Flats. The crew then drove the Popple Flats to no avail, but in the Pine Stump Drive, Ryan shot an 8-pointer from Steve's stand.

Eric immediately recognized the deer as the one that almost got him. We then crossed the river and swamped out the shack.

A good, but strange season. Lots of missed time. Four deer in total. Brown, warm and crunchy conditions are tough in the land of the Barking Spider Lodge.

This season we did have a treat in so far as an ancient photo of our deer camp that Paul R. brought out. He's guessing it's from 1960 or so and shows all of the "old blood" when they were young. We know their ghosts still hunt our forests and watch over us, but I wish they would visit us in our dreams and teach us a thing or two about killing bucks!

Saturday, November 26, 2011

Rain overnight, 42 degrees. Eric, Ryan, Steve, Russ, Tom, Matt, Josh, Noah and Mark S. crossed the river after being fortified by Steve's scrambled eggs and Tom's Happy Hog sausage.

Tom missed a Bullwinkle in the First Drive; later, Matt did the same with a smaller buck. Eric missed a 4- or 6-pointer during the Popple Flats Drive.

The crew then returned to the shack to swamp it out and head for home. Two bucks, three does for the season.

Steve buried his ATV and trailer with Russ on the highline going out in the rain. Not to be outdone, Eric tipped his trailer and load over on the road. Good times!

THE MAN-I-DO-WISH HUNT CLUB

In 1994, when I was editor of Wisconsin Outdoor Journal magazine, I was given permission to study the camp log and view the photos of the Man-i-do-wish Hunting Club, whose members hunted northern Wisconsin during the late 19th and early 20th centuries. The priceless collection was entrusted to me by Harvey B. Crane III of Fort Lauderdale, Florida, the grandson of the camp's patriarch. The article that followed is reprinted here because such information should be preserved and not lost to the march of time.

"Novermber is the proper month for Wisconsin." Given the craze of deer hunting that takes hold of this state each November, perhaps no more fitting words have ever been written. Yet they were penned in 1921 by an aging deer hunter by the name of Harvey B. Crane.

Crane was the secretary of the Man-i-do-wish Hunting Club, which organized in 1887 and continued in its original form until 1934. At that time it was believed to be the oldest hunting club in the United States. Crane's writings chronicled Wisconsin deer hunting history, beginning when Civil War veterans were part of the club and ending as Wisconsin's conservation ethic began to evolve. And his photographs, some of which appear on these pages, are easily worth a thousand words apiece.

In many ways the Man-i-do-wish Hunting Club was like deer camps today, but in many ways it was different. Often the glue that holds a camp together is a patriarch, and in the case of the Man-i-do-wish club it was Harvey Crane. He kept the old traditions and stories alive as age and other factors brought about a complete turnover of the names and faces of the members.

Crane's writings over 47 years are too voluminous to reproduce in their entirety. This synopsis of stories and quotations will have to suffice, but should be enough to give us a view of what turn-of-the-20th-century deer camps were all about. Crane's words capture the mystique of deer camp, the excitement of the hunt, the wonderment of inventions like automobiles and semi-automatic rifles, and the worries of everyday life that were left on the camp's doorstep.

THE CAMP

The name, Man-i-do-wish, was a derivation of the Chippewa tongue, meaning "deer trail of the woods," Crane explained. He continued, "It is capable under their mode of speaking, of a more or less forcible meaning, as are many others of their forms of expression. Thus, simply spoken, it has its simple meaning, but if expressed much more forcibly, with a lofty spreading gesture of the hands and a prolonged accent on the syllable 'do,' it then would mean the 'great deer trail of the woods.' To this latter form we now freely accord the preference in memory of the triumphs of our hunt."

For the most part, members came from outside of Wisconsin. Civil War veteran L.S. Van Vliet, the club's founding president, was a broker from Chicago. Crane was a lumberman who hailed from Wilson, Wisconsin, and later operated the Galloway House hotel in Eau Claire. Other original members were Charles Paulk of St. Paul, Minnesota, and H.R. Nelson of Lena, Illinois. Guests the first year included Nelson's son, Roy; T.M. Jackson of Chicago; Will Dean of St. Paul; J.H. Dunn of Lena; and Dr. S.L. Pickett of Wilson. Captain Ray Page of Bruce, Wisconsin, served as "guide" in the club's early years, making the necessary pre-hunt arrangements, organizing the hunts and running the hounds. Membership fees were $5, with $5 annual dues, increasing to $25 for new members and $10 annual dues by the club's end.

The camp had a number of hunting sites, beginning on the Flambeau River north of present-day Ladysmith. At the time, Ladysmith was known as "Deer Tail," and Crane said it consisted of "a few frame and log houses, a small saw mill, blacksmith shop, store, saloon and tavern."

"Little Farm," "Little Falls," and "Beaver Dam Falls" were the original homes of what they called Camp Page, on the Flambeau. As settlers began to increase in number near Camp Page, club members spent several years looking for a new home, finally choosing what they called Camp Mooch-a-bout, roughly two miles south of Lake Namekagon in southern Bayfield County, in 1912.

Travel was difficult — club members traveled by rail or horse-drawn wagon along muddy logging roads into camp in the days before automobiles. Crane wrote about one frustrating trip into camp when the "[horse] team could not get used to the frequent flushing of partridge, and every time it happened they would shy." In 1904, as the age of automobiles neared, Crane recorded the following discussion by two guests of the camp: "A little later, Andy told about a new automobile that had made its appearance in Chicago. That roused Harry, who was in the vehicle business, and he cut loose, 'I'm still of the opinion that this horseless rig is pretty much of a fad, and will run its course just like the bicycle craze. Why, just look at the price they want for the contraption, and their terms. Besides that, they demand cash on the nail before shipment'." It wasn't many years before the first cars appeared in camp.

CAMP LIFE

A number of camp rules were enforced. "We had agreed for the sake of harmony in camp that gambling, political and religious discussions should be taboo, which was strictly adhered to until (Grover) Cleveland's first election," Crane wrote. A sheet of paper with the rules of gun safety was tacked to the door of the camp so that members were reminded every time they entered the building. In the days of red and black plaid mackinaw jackets, when a number of hunters across the state died every year because of accidental shootings, Man-i-do-wish members did not suffer a single injury because of unsafe gun use.

Eating was a big part of camps Page and Mooch-a-bout. The club hired camp cooks to prepare all their meals, the most popular chef being "Namekagon George" Curtis. A typical breakfast included pork sausage, fresh walleye, buckwheat pancakes and maple syrup, and the cook at Camp Page once remarked, "When you are tired of fresh pike [walleye] tell me, we've plenty of venison, ham, bacon and sausage." An annual hunters' banquet was started in 1912 in honor of Roy Farwell, a member who, just before getting to camp, received a telegram calling him away on urgent business. When he was able to get to camp with a few days remaining in the season, he was greeted with the banquet, which was so popular it became a tradition. Banquet menus were handscribed on birch bark and later bore hand-painted camp scenes.

Entertainment and camaraderie were important to the Man-i-do-wish hunters. There were camp songs such as "Marching Through Georgia" and "Flambeau River." Besides singing, a gramophone was used for several years and in the 1920s, radio debuted in camp.

Anyone who has spent a few days in a deer camp knows that great pleasure is derived from high jinks. In 1893, with conser-

Camp Page

vation thinking leaning heavily against predators, a lynx and a badger were killed, then posed by a photographer as if ready to do battle over a dead rabbit. C.D. Moon "saved" Dr. E.F. Sommermeyer from a "wounded" buck in another camp photo from 1917 (the buck, by this point, had already been gutted and frozen into position). Another camp member known for shooting at ravens was set up by other campmates who shot a raven and wired it to a tree at a pre-arranged lunch site. Only after shooting several times with no effect did the shooter realize he had been duped.

An annual shooting match was held in high regard with a badge awarded to the top sharpshooter. Marksmanship was valued by the Man-i-do-wish Hunting Club but it wasn't always achieved. "It seems the buck came straight at Jim, who (as usual) missed but his shot turned the buck towards Harry who stopped him," Crane wrote after one hunt.

ON THE HUNT

Though camp life has been reported thus far, it was the hunting that drew members back year after year. The Man-i-do-wish hunters were largely successful, killing seven deer in a drive in 1902 and five in a 1914 drive. In 1917, Crane recorded, "We secured our complement of deer easily, picking them for size, and largely bucks." These animals were shot from hunting areas known as "Balsam Avenue," "Crane's Corners," "Wildcat Narrows" and the "Hair Pin."

The excitement of a first buck was not lost in Crane's writings. "A few minutes later the sharp crack of a rifle in the direction of camp was heard, followed by loud shouts, 'Page, Page, I've shot a big buck'. Page happened to be within ear shot and was soon on the scene to find the kid dancing wildly about a splendid buck. As soon as he saw Page, he ran to meet him yelling, 'You told me you'd put me where I could shoot a buck, and I did.' ... Page interjected, 'He made a dead center shot right between the eyes, he's a chip off the old block, all right.'

"Harry, had an investigating turn of mind, and he wanted to know all the details, and from this on down through the years about every deer that was shot, the shooter was put through the sprouts of a rigid cross examination, which often gave us a lot of amusement."

Curiously, there is little reference in Crane's writings to the size of the antlers on the bucks the camp bagged. There was considerable mention of the size of the deer, with bucks being labeled as big as an ox, jersey cow or elephant. In 1900, camp members debated the myth that you can tell the age of a buck by the number of its points, a belief that for the most part, thankfully, has been put to rest.

In the late 1800s there was no bag limit on deer, though eventually a 2-deer limit was instituted. Until 1898 it was legal to drive deer with dogs. The Man-i-do-wish hunters used hounds through the 1901 season, when a game warden's threat caused them to change their ways.

There's nothing like a good debate over "Why I Like My Rifle And I Think Yours Is Junk" to liven up any deer camp. The evolution of the modern rifle occurred during the days of the Man-i-do-wish Hunting Club and was duly recorded by Crane. In 1895 a camp member brought the first Winchester .38-55 into

Camp Mooch-a-bout

camp, which was eyed with keen interest by the other members, who used the Winchester .40-82.

In 1900 the now-famous Winchester Model 94 in .30-30 caliber was introduced to the camp, and some members viewed the rifle with skepticism, calling it a "popgun." Crane noted, "A sweet little gun that filled our eyes at once. Our club to a man had always been Winchester fans fancying octagon barrels with Kentucky stocks. But this little arm came on the market in round barrels and shot gun stocks. Which at that time seemed to be a serious objection to us. However, moth like we kept fluttering about them, and finally each of us bought one."

Semi-automatics were due on the scene shortly. In 1907, guest Frank Trump told the campmates that he had been to Denver earlier that year and "he called on Mr. Browning, the famed gun inventor, and was shown a wonder gun that he had completed, and which he had made arrangements with the Winchester company to manufacture and market. The gun is a wide departure in principle from any other rifle. The action being entirely automatic, and would deliver six shots as fast as one could press the trigger ... there is to be two calibers to start with, .405 and .351 ..."

By 1912 the first semi-automatic rifles were purchased, all .351-caliber.

Man-i-do-wish members occasionally had difficulties with gummed firing pins. In 1926, it was recorded, "that night the trouble was discovered, namely, the intense cold frosted the guns, and fetched into the warm atmosphere of the camp the frost condensed covering the guns with moisture, during the night the heat dried them off nicely on the outside, but unfortunately there was enough moisture left in the mechanism, and as soon as the rifles came in contact with freezing temperature, this moisture again congealed, and the firing pins could not be driven with sufficient force to explode the shells, hence the awful debacle. The event led to much and loud explosive talk that night, and there was no danger of it occurring again, you bet." A remedy Crane wrote about occasionally was to put a few drops of kerosene on the firing pin, which acted as a solvent and removed gunk and moisture.

Though the Man-i-do-wish Hunting Club's meatpole never seemed to be at a loss for deer in any one season, the Wisconsin legislature began debate over the "one-buck law," which allowed each hunter to kill one buck with no antlerless take. In 1913 Crane noted from the camp's discussions: "... the hunters are strongly opposed to it," and "I had heard some talk about it, but always there seemed to be so much opposition it hadn't bothered me." By 1915, however, the 1-buck law passed, though it was in and out of effect several times in the next few years.

OTHER MATTERS

The realities of World War I infringed upon the peace of Camp Mooch-a-bout. Crane was a bit more upbeat regarding the war and its effects on the United States in 1914 than in 1919. In 1914 he wrote, "Europe may be busy cutting their own throats, but the Man-i-do-wish Club must have its annual hunt

The club's meatpole hangs heavy with venison.

nonetheless." By 1919 he had this to say: "The aftermath of the great war is making itself very seriously felt. Demoralization stalks abroad on every side and in the middle. Labor commands a premium. Wages outrageous and duties shirked. Brawn taking the place of brains, at least were remuneration is concerned, and we wonder what the fates have in store for us."

Wisconsin's legislature closed the deer season in 1925 and in odd-numbered years thereafter through 1935 in a misguided attempt to "stockpile" deer and increase the herd. This lack of continuity in the hunting season, the advancing age of some of the members, and the Great Depression probably combined to bring about the end of Camp Mooch-a-bout and the Man-i-do-wish Hunting Club.

On April 21, 1934, a special meeting was held to address the club's future. With unpaid taxes and insurance, an unpaid balance on a promissory note, and camp buildings falling into disrepair, it was decided to accept an offer of $400 for the camp and grounds with the purchaser assuming all debts.

In July of that year the club was reorganized as the Man-i-do-wish Hunting and Fishing Club, with 84-year-old Harvey Crane receiving an honorary membership. As was his custom with the original club, Crane served as secretary at the first meeting of the new club.

Crane wrote: "The chronicler hereof, wishes that the future of the new club, will be as full of happy successful hunts, freedom from accidents, as those so keenly enjoyed by the parent club, during its 47 years active career, and leave behind as many glorious memories."

WHITETAILS THAT WERE SMARTER THAN ME

Although it happened nearly twenty years ago, the big buck that eluded me that November day continues to haunt my memories.

I was still-hunting along the top of a ravine when a red squirrel chattered in the valley below. Back then, an abundance of fishers following their reintroduction into northern Wisconsin made red squirrels a scarce commodity in our hunting territory. If one was angry enough to let its presence be known I felt the situation was worth checking out. I peeked over the edge of the ravine and was startled to see a giant buck lunge forward. I found him in my scope and just as I was about to squeeze the trigger the buck turned to climb the far side of the ravine, my view suddenly blocked by a large spruce.

As if he had planned it that way, the buck kept the spruce between him and me, quickly topped the ravine and was gone — I never did get a shot at what was one of the largest bucks I have ever seen.

It sometimes seems like deer have a sixth sense that warns them of looming danger, but my hunting buddies would gladly explain this phenomenon by pointing out deer are simply smarter than me. Here are stories of some more encounters that may prove they are right.

I was having one of those years when nothing was going

right, and the season was nearing a close as my deer camp conducted a drive. I held an antlerless tag in my pocket and wanted a doe to eat, and strained my eyes and ears for any sign of an approaching deer. To the east was posted one of my hunting buddies, and when the drive ended and we got together to walk out, he asked "Why didn't you shoot that deer?" I hadn't seen anything, but Paul insisted that a doe had walked up to me from behind before eventually wandering off. He couldn't shoot it for safety reasons, but I never heard nor saw it, though I was told it stood no more than 30 yards behind me.

One October I was hunting a special antlerless season and watched a fawn feed its way along the edge of the ridge upon which I sat. I spotted a doe picking her way along the top of the ridge toward me, occasionally looking at her fawn. When her head went behind a large pine tree I lifted my rifle and waited for her to step out, but the doe stopped. I could see her back half but nothing else as seconds turned to minutes and my rifle grew heavy. Suddenly, she turned and ran 20 yards, stopped behind some brush and eventually walked away, never offering me a shot.

In early November one year I had just settled into my tree stand when I heard deer moving toward me. I attached my release to my bowstring and watched a wide, white-racked 8-pointer thread its way through nearby balsams. A couple of fawns followed their mother to the top of the ridge where they milled about. The doe continued over the ridge toward a swamp on the far side.

I came to full draw on the buck, but two steps from an opening that would put him in a shooting lane and a mere ten paces from the base of my tree, he stopped, picked his head up, and looked over his shoulder at the doe. The buck stood for what seemed like minutes but I know was only seconds, turned in place and followed the doe. Together they faded away into the woods and forever out of my life.

Because the fall months are considered prime time for big muskies, I stopped bow-hunting for about 20 years. During that time, the rattling technique went from being considered a Texas phenomenon to something that worked regularly for hunters throughout the deer world. When I started bow-hunting again I bought a rattle bag and practiced often, though I don't really think my technique was any better than when I first took it out of its packaging. Never mind that the first deer I rattled in was a doe fawn. Anyway, later that fall I was perched 18 feet up an oak tree on the edge of a swamp and was more or less pinned down for a half-hour by a doe that loitered in the area but was somewhat suspicious of the camouflaged lump hanging from the tree. When she disappeared into the swamp, I pulled out the rattle bag and shook the woods with the sounds of battle.

Minutes later I spotted a deer coming from the direction the doe had gone and I wondered why she was coming back. The deer stepped into a natural opening, and I spotted a nice 8-point rack and realized I had rattled in my first buck. I gripped my bow a little tighter and watched the buck cautiously pick its way to the edge of the swamp and then stop, less than 30 yards away, in cover I couldn't even hope to thread an arrow through. That buck stood for nearly 20 minutes watching the woods around my tree before he turned and wandered off.

My hunting buddies and I used to joke that if we ever knew how many deer eluded us we would quit the sport. Now, thanks to trail cameras, we do. Nobody I know has yet given up because of what they have discovered on their cameras, but I will admit to my share of frustration.

One fall a pair of big bucks — an 8-pointer and a

9-pointer — showed up on my trail camera during the rut, but they always came through at night. I was thrilled because previously I was unaware of either buck and had seen only smaller animals on my camera or from my stand prior to the rut. Either of the bucks would look good on my living room wall, I figured. They were dandies.

Early bow season came and went, and as gun season gave way to late bow season I was delighted when my camera revealed the 8-pointer was still in the neighborhood, but again, he came through only at night. Then came the December Sunday afternoon when the wind was perfect for my stand and I planned to hunt, but at the last moment chose to stay in the comfort of my living room and watch the Green Bay Packers beat the Chicago Bears. The outcome of the game was exactly as I hoped as the Packers won handily, but ... well, you guessed it. Two days later when I checked my camera I discovered the 8-pointer had not only walked down the trail my camera overlooked while I was watching the game, but it had loitered in the area for about 12 minutes. Two days after that my camera revealed the buck had shed its antlers.

While the author watched the Packers beat the Bears, a buck he had hunted all season was visiting his stand.

The following December I still had an unfilled bow tag and decided to hunt the waning days of the season on an oak-covered ridge that was still laced with acorns. The snow was starting to pile up but pawings in the snow indicated the deer were having no trouble finding the preferred food source. When my trail camera showed that a respectable 7-pointer was regularly feeding on the ridge during daylight hours, I figured it was only a matter of time before he went home with me.

Two weeks later it was painfully obvious that the buck had my number. On the days when I didn't hunt he paraded past my camera during the day; when I hunted, I didn't see him. If I hunted in the morning, he came through in the afternoon. When I hunted the afternoon, he wandered through in the morning. My guess is he bedded in a location where he either could see or hear me when I parked my truck or walked to the stand. In fact, there were a couple instances when he walked past my camera within an hour of my leaving.

Eventually that bow-hunting season came to an end with the buck still alive. He deserved to survive the season, because I had no answer for him. He really may have been smarter than me.

MY 2009 DEER HUNT, AND WELCOME TO IT

As long as I live I will never forget how my 2009 season ended. I slogged out of the darkening December woods, dragging my bow as well as my posterior, wondering just what it would take to kill a deer that year. It had been that kind of season.

Remember the movie "Groundhog Day"? In it, supernatural forces conspire to keep Bill Murray stuck on February 2 until he has changed his life and won the affections of co-star Andie MacDowell. Well, there's no love story involved in my deer hunting but it did seem like forces beyond my control were working against me.

The purpose of this chapter is not to blame anyone or anything for the fact that I did not kill a single deer during the bow, gun and muzzleloader seasons in Wisconsin as well as an out-of-state muzzleloader hunt. Rather, my point in writing this chapter is for others to have fun at my expense. I scouted hard and hunted harder and saw lots of deer, but I still ended my fall eating tag stew.

To paraphrase Winston Churchill, "Never before has anyone hunted so hard to have killed so little."

The season started almost magnificently. I had seen a big 8-point buck several times in the same general location in August, so I placed a scouting camera on a trail he used to confirm his late summer pattern. In fact, on the day I set out the camera I found one of the buck's sheds from the previous year. When the buck showed up on photos taken by my trail cam, I knew precisely where I would sit when bow season opened.

The second day of the bow season that September was unusually warm but I hunted anyway, knowing the wind was right and the buck's patterns could change any day. As the light and legal shooting time faded away, I heard a deer walking behind me. I peeked over my left shoulder and there he was, head down, feeding on acorns next to a stump I'd already ranged at 22 yards. However, he was facing me ... with a rifle the season would have been over quickly, but with a bow I needed to wait for a better shot. I turned my head slowly and waited, and waited, until I knew there were mere minutes left to hunt. I chanced another look over my shoulder and he caught the movement, and with a single bound he was swallowed up by the swamp. He stopped, snorted at me once, and was gone.

I caught him on the trail camera two more times that week but then he disappeared. I did not see him again the remainder of the fall or, for that matter, ever again.

Late September produced a remarkable evening when I watched four yearling bucks walk by within range, but nothing of the size I wanted to shoot. Then came the evening of September 29. It was 65 degrees when I parked my truck, but after I had climbed into my stand a thunderstorm blew through and soaked me thoroughly. The temperature fell as the skies cleared and I started to shiver, badly. With an hour left to hunt I knew I could not make it until darkness, so I climbed down and walked out.

A hundred yards from my truck I jumped a doe and two fawns. During the couple-mile drive home my truck's onboard thermometer indicated the air temperature had plummeted to 49 degrees. I also saw nine more does and fawns — the deer were moving and I feared the worst. Two days later when I checked my trail camera my suspicions were confirmed — before shooting hours ended and while I was driving home, two bucks with antlers big enough for me had walked past the stand I had vacated.

October faded into November, and though I saw deer most evenings the hunt was largely unremarkable. Curiously, it was Friday, November 13, when I rattled in a big 8-pointer but he stayed in the thick stuff and never offered a shot. I later heard him rubbing his antlers on a bush and I blew my grunt tube at him, but then it got dark.

During an out-of-state muzzleloader hunt I had seen only does and fawns through the first two days, but on the third day I was delighted to spot a 9-pointer walking toward my shooting lane. As his head entered the shooting lane and I brought my muzzleloader up to shoot, the buck abruptly stopped and raised his head, looked slightly to his right, and then turned and bolted back the way he had come. I was dumbfounded, but blew my grunt tube in the hope of bringing the buck back. It didn't work. A minute or so later, I heard what proved to be a truck grinding its way in low range up the steep, rocky logging road that I had used for access to this stand. Hollywood couldn't have timed it better — I was seconds from pulling the trigger when the noise of the truck spooked the buck. Now, it hurts to drive an ATV on this trail, but here was some other hunter driving a 4-wheel-drive pickup on it and the buck didn't like it.

I never saw another deer on that hunt because the next day a warm front blew in and the high temperature each day was 50-plus degrees. Daytime deer movement ceased.

It was a bucks-only Wisconsin gun season at both my

camp in Ashland County as well as my home zone in Vilas County. Naturally I saw only does at camp. Returning home for the final day, I was delighted to wake up to two inches of new-fallen snow and headed out to still-hunt a clearcut. Rounding a corner I spotted a deer about a hundred yards away. I dialed up my scope and ... it was a doe. A second deer stepped out as well as a third, and they too were bald.

A 10-day muzzleloader season immediately follows Wisconsin's 9-day gun season and, one evening, I felt my efforts would finally be rewarded. They weren't. The buck I spotted just out of range disappeared without offering a shot.

Which leads me to my late bow-hunting outing mentioned in the opening paragraph. I had come to the conclusion I would try to kill any adult deer that showed itself, and then call it a season. It was a cold December, in fact the high was only 18 degrees that day, and the snow was getting deep. Shortly after climbing into my stand, two big does fed down the trail and with the wind in my face they had no clue I was watching from about 20 yards away. I drew, centered the sight pin on the heart of the biggest deer, and when I squeezed the release I was shocked to watch my arrow elevate and glance off the top of her back. It was a shot I had made a thousand times that year while practicing from a tree stand in my back-yard, but I couldn't make it when it counted most. Looking around in dismay, I spotted the fall-away rest of my bow still in its upright position. It was frozen in place — certainly the reason I'd missed ... but come on.

I climbed from my tree and walked to where the doe stood and found that I'd cut hair off the top of her back, but only a single blade of the mechanical broadhead was deployed and no blood showed on the arrow. I dutifully followed the trail for 200 yards and never found any blood. So, I climbed back into my tree stand and soon it was dark.

169

It's not like people around me didn't bag deer that year. My son shot his biggest buck; a friend killed three dandies — one each with his bow and rifle, and another in Canada; and another friend hunted for a total of seven hours and arrowed a buck and a doe, and killed a 150-inch 10-pointer on Opening Day of Wisconsin's gun season. The wife of a buddy killed a buck with her bow that measured just shy of the Boone & Crockett qualifying score. Ask them about the 2009 deer season and you will hear some amazing stuff.

But not from me. The nearly four months I hunted that fall were certainly remarkable, but not for the reasons I had hoped. That's the story of my 2009 deer hunting season, and you're welcome to it.

2010'S SEASON OF MISSTEPS

If not for a nice 10-point buck that I killed during an out-of-state muzzleloader hunt in 2010, I would have been highly suspicious that the dark clouds that hung over my 2009 deer hunts had followed into the new year. I have added this sub-chapter about the first four days of the 2010 gun deer season in Wisconsin — as well as the day before opener — because nothing went right in almost the same crazy way as they had the year before.

On the day before the opener I always meet up with a couple of my fellow camp members and do the grocery shopping for the week, then haul everything out to our remote shack with ATVs and trailers. It's nearly a 2-hour drive from my home to camp, and 20 minutes into my trip I realized I had forgotten the batch of chili I had prepared for dinner that night. So, I turned around to get the chili, and called one of the guys to tell him I would be late. No worries, I just met up with the guys at the grocery store.

The next day was Opening Day. While overlooking a river

bottom and eating a candy bar for energy, I chipped a tooth. As the day progressed we found that few deer were moving, so my camp members and I gathered in the early afternoon with the intent of making a drive or two to get the deer on their feet. Posted as a stander in a tree stand, I was delighted to see a 6-point buck walking my way. In many of the deer camps of northern Wisconsin, the unwritten code is that if someone makes the effort to drive to you and pushes out a buck, you kill it regardless of its antler size. Well, the buck stepped into an opening 40 yards away and I squeezed the trigger and watched the buck kick up and disappear. I figured it was down.

As I scanned the woods for more deer, I was shocked to see the buck I had just shot at still on its feet and walking. I fired again and the buck disappeared into the brush. When the drive ended a bunch of us spent a considerable amount of time looking unsuccessfully for sign of a hit. We did find where my first bullet had plowed into the earth and where the second had clipped a pine tree, but there was no indication the deer was harmed. I speculated the first shot had been deflected by an unseen branch and the second had obviously been knocked askew by the tree; after all, I had just shot the rifle on the range the week before the season and knew the scope was on.

The next day was Sunday and most everyone leaves camp for home and a shower at the end of the day. Since I live a considerable distance from camp, I was invited to spend the evening at the home of one of my camp partners. Leaving camp that night my ATV broke down. By flashlight, I jerry-rigged the machine, and eventually I reached where I had parked my truck.

There, I found a back tire was nearly flat. With it already being dark and the ground soft and muddy, I chose to limp into town where I pumped the tire up at a gas station, rather than change it in the field. I then drove to my friend's house where we changed the tire in his heated and well-lit garage.

The following morning was Monday. My ATV required a field-fix again on the way to camp, and as dawn broke I was in a tree stand on the edge of an old clearcut. A couple hours later I spotted a respectable 8-point buck heading my way, and when he stepped into an opening I squeezed the trigger. The buck jumped up, looked around, and I put the crosshairs on his shoulder and fired again. He bolted for the clearcut where he disappeared, and I figured he was down. As I scanned through my scope for sign of the buck I was stunned to see it peeking around a tree, still very much in charge of its faculties. When it stepped out from the tree I fired again and the deer ran off.

I climbed out of the stand and walked to where the buck was standing for my first two shots, but there was no sign he had been hit. I followed the buck's tracks to where I fired my third shot and again, there was no sign of a hit. Now, fearing my scope was off and angry at the whole situation, I stomped back to camp and placed a target on a tree. Three shots confirmed my suspicions — at 42 yards (the distance from my stand to the buck) my scope was nine inches low! How, when or why it was knocked out of alignment remains anybody's guess. I sighted the gun back in.

The next day, Tuesday, found me in the same tree stand before dawn and, when I checked my watch at 4:05 in the afternoon, I had yet to see a deer. I was cold but happy I had lasted all day, and figured I deserved to have something good happen in the last half-hour of shooting light. That's when the wolves started to howl. Close. Though I never saw them I guessed they were within a quarter-mile of my stand, which was confirmed the next day by tracks in the snow. Needless to say I did not see a deer that evening.

The remainder of the season was uneventful. Sure I had to make a couple of field-fixes on my ATV, but since I already knew how to do it I am through whining about it. When darkness fell on the last day of the gun-hunting season I had not killed a deer.

The author with the buck he and Kevin Schmidt called "Stickers."

THE HUNT FOR "STICKERS"

We first became aware of the buck we would eventually nickname "Stickers" in October 2010 when my buddy, Kevin, and I checked trail cameras that overlooked stands we had placed a long way back in the woods prior to an out-of-state hunt.

"Holy cow, Steve! Look at this one!" Kevin shouted as he scrolled through the photos contained on the memory chip he had pulled from the camera at his stand. I just about put my truck in the ditch trying to pull over to the side so I could look at the photos, but the images I saw that day were worth the risk.

A large, swayback buck carried 13 points on a 6x5 rack that had a G-5 on the left antler and two sticker points rising up out of one antler's burr. The wide rack wasn't particularly heavy, but given what we knew about bucks in the area, we estimated him to be 4½ to 5½ years old, a real trophy. However, all of the photos we had were taken at night. And, curiously, though my stand was a half-mile as the crow flies from Kevin's stand, and other bucks had visited both of our stands since we'd placed the cameras, Stickers had not. When he showed, it was in the middle of the night at Kevin's stand.

Both Kevin and I shot good bucks that year and Stickers continued to show up on Kevin's camera, but at night. In what we knew of Stickers' world, my stand and daylight hours did not exist. We left the woods that fall pleased with the knowledge that a buck of Stickers' caliber was around, yet we wondered if the buck might be unkillable. A big, old buck, in an area as far back in the woods as we have ever hunted, in a place where human contact would be minimal if it even occurred at all, yet he would not show himself during the day.

Two weeks after we placed our trail cameras overlooking the same stand sites in 2011, Stickers appeared again. However, he had regressed somewhat and carried a smaller 10-point rack, with his G-5 and stickers gone, yet the shape of his antlers and body were unmistakable. We wondered if he was not older than we thought and on the downhill slide. With his swayback, he just looked old, and he kept up his practice of avoiding my stand and showing up at Kevin's at night. Again, Kevin and I each shot a good buck, but we did not have any encounters with Stickers.

Which leads us to 2012. Again, as in 2010, we had just checked our stands and Kevin was reviewing his photos as I drove. "Steve, he's got points all over his face!" Now, I have fished and hunted with Kevin on countless trips in some of the

A trail camera photo of Stickers in 2010.

best destinations in North America, yet I could count on one hand the number of times I have seen him really shook up about something, and have fingers left over. This was one of those times.

Kevin's photos revealed that Stickers had "blown up" since 2011. His body was bigger and there was that same swayback look. His antlers swept out and upward in a large 5x5 rack, but he had a cluster of points rising up between the burr and G-1 on his left antler. "I've shot spike bucks with antlers shorter than the points in that cluster," I joked. We tried counting all the points, and it appeared Stickers now had 14.

Again, he was at Kevin's stand only, yet one time he showed during legal shooting hours. Was this a chink in his armor? Could it be possible we could take a buck that was now two years older and wiser, two years after we had discussed the likelihood of him being unkillable? Sleep did not come easily that evening.

Opening Day found me on stand, not the one near Kevin but about four miles away. The wind was not right for my other stand, but it was good for Kevin's. He watched several does but

Stickers regressed somewhat in 2011, with fewer overall points and no stickers.

did not see a buck. I saw a spike buck and three does, and was delighted to watch four ruffed grouse feeding on buds in the popples around me. The spike, a doe, and the partridge showed up right around moonrise that afternoon.

The wind changed direction overnight. It was still good for Kevin's stand, and it was perfect for my stand near his, so that was where I went. Arriving in the pre-dawn darkness, I changed the memory chip in my trail camera and found its counter displaying 178 photos having been taken in the 42 hours since I had last visited. After settling into my stand and pulling on my heavy clothing, I checked my watch and found I had another 45 minutes until legal shooting light. With plenty of time, I inserted the chip into my point-and-shoot camera and started scrolling through the photos.

"Stickers was here last night!" I breathed as photo after photo showed the giant buck. Besides Stickers, the stand site was visited by a large 10-pointer, a giant 8-pointer, another 8-pointer that I considered big enough to shoot, a forkhorn, and numerous does. According to my trail camera, only the two 8-pointers had ever visited that stand before, and Stickers and

A photo taken the night before he died shows Stickers "blew up" in 2012.

the 10-pointer were new. Something happened that night, I surmised ... quite possibly a doe had come into heat.

Legal shooting light could not come soon enough. I reasoned I would kill the 10-pointer that day because Stickers was unkillable, and the two 8-pointers had been there before. You see, I think a big buck is like a big musky in that it is most vulnerable the first day or two after it shows up on a spot. After it gets acclimated to its surroundings, everything must be perfect for you to succeed.

Daylight came, and so did a button buck, and again, and again, and again. Four times that morning the button buck wandered through, but nothing else. The fact a fawn was by itself underscores my belief that a doe had come into heat the night before — its mother was being bred by a buck during that time.

Pretty soon daylight was fading fast, and with about a half-hour to go in legal shooting time I spotted a deer picking its way through the jackpines. I could not see much of it but I could tell it was bigger than the button buck, and when I saw a flash of antler my heart started racing.

Another view the night before Stickers died.

I had a high definition video camera on a tripod aimed in the buck's direction, and I turned it on hoping to catch the action. Five minutes later, the buck still had not stepped out, and my hands, knees and lower lip trembled. Finally, its head eased into a shooting lane and I spotted two tiny antlers — the forkhorn!

There I sat, shaking, and laughing at myself because I was going to pieces over a buck I had no intention of killing. Still, I noticed the forkie had an air of nervousness about him, and he kept looking off to his right. Could there be another deer coming? After two minutes, the forkhorn backed out and left.

I glanced at my watch and saw that only 10 minutes of legal shooting time remained. I checked the viewfinder of the video camera to see if there was sufficient light and battery power to keep it running for the final few minutes, and I spotted something dark move between the trees through the viewfinder.

Instantly I eased my .30-06 forward on its shooting stick and peered through the scope. Without much time left I knew I would have to shoot immediately if the deer was a buck that I wanted. Through the scope I spotted a large deer, and when it stepped from behind a pine trunk into a shooting lane I recognized a large antler. Was he looking for the doe that had caused the ruckus the night before? At the moment, I did not care why though I have pondered that question ever since. I eased the safety off, settled the crosshairs on the buck's opposite shoulder, and the rifle jumped as I squeezed the trigger.

The buck shuddered as it absorbed the hit, and then collapsed where it had stood. It kicked once, then twice, and was still. I dialed my scope up to 7-power and saw a large antler rising off the right side of its head and mused that the 10-pointer had a bigger rack than I had originally thought. I zoomed in with the video camera but that did not reveal any more than my scope had.

I got up and walked through the shooting lane toward the buck. The right antler seemed to grow as I got closer, and soon I saw that a small tree branch and a dip in the ground were blocking my view of the left antler. I touched the buck's eye to make sure it was dead, and lifted the right antler. Immediately I saw the cluster of points at the base of the left antler.

It was Stickers!

Kneeling, I laid my rifle to the side and started counting points. It is funny how you remember the oddest things when you're excited, and I immediately thought of my friend, Paul Bietka, as he tried counting the 16 points on a giant buck he had killed while posted on a drive many years before at our deer camp. I was the first driver on the scene as Paul walked up to his buck, and he and I had to touch each point as we counted to get every one. That is what I did with Stickers, and my count ended at 15 — a 5x5 with five stickers on the left side.

I looked at the giant buck and wondered what I would tell Kevin. I was excited, yet somehow I had always thought of Stickers as *his* buck. After all, it only visited his stand. I unloaded my rifle, gave thanks to my Creator, and affixed my tag

Stickers, where he fell.

to its antler. That's when I heard the rumble of Kevin's ATV as it came up the logging road out of the drainage.

I carried my rifle and heavy coat out to where I had parked my ATV, and met Kevin. "I got Stickers!" I blurted (so much for finding the right words), but it did not register immediately with my friend because he had not heard me shoot. "I got Stickers. He's a 15-pointer!"

Kevin and I walked back to where Stickers lay. The giant buck was right where I had left him; only a few snow flurries had fallen on his still form. Kevin shook my hand and pounded me on the back. We admired the heavy rack and giant body, took some pictures, field-dressed him, and dragged Stickers to my ATV.

I do not recall what was said that evening as we told the tales of our hunts. My excitement of the moment did a fine job of blurring my memory. I do know, however, that Kevin never once said anything that would lead me to believe he was disappointed that I was the one who killed Stickers, and not him. Maybe that is the sign of a true friend, or maybe it is a sign that I'm a lesser man for even thinking that.

The next day Stickers weighed 208 pounds. Without telling him what we knew about the buck, I asked the taxidermist to look at the wear on Stickers' teeth and estimate his age. The taxidermist's best guess for Stickers was at least 6½ years old and probably 7½, which fit exactly with our best guess. After drying, the antlers scored 178⅝ inches, with main beams measuring more than 25 inches.

For those of you who may doubt my beliefs of the moon's effect on deer, consider Stickers was shot on the day of the full moon, about an hour after it had risen, during what John Alden Knight's Solunar Tables would call a "Minor." A coincidence perhaps, but when you see things like this happen time and again you begin to believe.

Stickers was a buck who lived in a place where man was only an occasional intruder. It's quite possible the only men he saw before he died were driving by in the cab of logging trucks. During his lifetime he had endured bone-chilling nights, waded through chest deep snow, had likely fought off or fled from wolves, had grown and shed some remarkable antlers, and, hopefully, had sired lots of little bucks that will someday take his place.

Stickers also taught this hunter to never, ever, rule out the possibility of something special happening in the northwoods. Unkillable bucks do make mistakes. By living, Stickers taught me to be a better hunter, and by dying, he taught me that hunting is a lot more fun when you have a great hunting partner.

TAKE WHAT MOTHER NATURE GIVES YOU

Winter can be cruel to the white-tailed deer, and the winter of 2012-13 was no exception. Slow to start through December, winter came on strong in January and continued to pile snow right into the middle of May. In some northern locales, the last of the snow didn't completely melt until June.

Biologists use a number of ways to measure a winter's impact on white-tailed deer, and by those parameters the winter didn't appear to be very severe. However, the extremely-late snow melt produced a different set of problems. When the higher sun of spring triggered the deer's metabolisms to ramp up and their diet to change, the environment around them didn't. Green-up came late, and the nourishment does need to feed their newborn fawns, and bucks need to begin packing on pounds and growing antlers, was slow to come.

Biologists tell us the first deer to die in a harsh winter are the older bucks, which enter winter already stressed by the rut, and the fawns. If this is happening, it is likely that some does will be stressed enough that their newborn fawns won't make it, either. Most hunters understood that deer were lost during the winter of 2012-13 but it wasn't until the following fall when the true scope of the damage became evident.

Bow-hunters in many locations saw it first when they simply didn't see large bucks, either with their eyes or in the images taken by their trail cameras. In some cases, bucks they knew about whose antlers sported unique characteristics carried stunted antlers, smaller than the year before.

It was against this scenario that I planned my annual out-of-state deer hunt. My usual partner for this hunt, Kevin Schmidt, was unable to go because of family reasons, but I decided to go by myself because this trip had been so good to us for so many years. Typically we travel to our hunting location two weeks prior to the actual hunt to set up stands and place trail cameras, and we often joke that we feel like kids at Christmas reviewing the trail cameras' photos when we return to hunt.

Although I figured the winter would have had some effect on the local deer, I was confident because the year before our trail cameras had captured photos of a number of nice bucks that we didn't get. Pressure from other hunters is negligible because this location is extremely remote and requires great effort to hunt, so my best guess was that there would still be a couple of good bucks around.

I was very wrong.

Upon arrival for the hunt I was surprised at the lack of rut sign at my stands. When I reviewed the photos taken by my trail cameras, I found that a stand where we had left three big bucks the year before now had a large-bodied 5-point buck with a goofy rack, a small 8-pointer, and a forkhorn, as well as does and fawns. The other stand I had set up — which the year before had twin 9-pointers with nearly identical racks — was only being visited by a forkhorn, and a single doe with twin fawns.

I was shocked. All of the big bucks I'd hoped to be hunting were gone. Briefly I was tempted to repack my truck and return home, and save my vacation days for something else. But then I realized I was hunting at the outset of the rut and that a big buck that had survived the winter could show up anytime. In the meantime, there was this 5-pointer ... reviewing the photos, I realized he actually was a pretty nice buck with a large body and antler frame. While he looked like he should have been a respectable 8- or 10-point buck, he had grown only three points on his left antler. The right side was simply a big fork. I had never seen a buck with antlers like this before, and decided that if I got a chance I would gladly take him.

This was the setting for what turned out to be possibly the most mentally-challenging hunt I've made. I had no one with whom to discuss the day's events, and as anyone who has hunted in a group knows, it's always a mental pick-me-up when someone has enjoyed action even when you have not. Fortunately, I had my trail cameras to record what was happening at the stands I wasn't hunting.

The deer, however, had other plans. High hopes on Saturday turned to darkness at the close of shooting hours on Tuesday as I had yet to see a deer. Even more shocking was that none of my cameras had recorded any daytime deer activity at the stands I wasn't hunting, nor were there any big bucks (though another small 8-pointer had walked by one stand around midnight on Sunday). I knew there weren't many deer to begin with and those that were left had pulled a grand disappearing act. I called my wife Tuesday night and told her that unless something good happened Wednesday, I would pull my stands and trail cameras that evening and return home Thursday. I am a glass-half-full sort of guy, but I admit I was on the verge of being beaten.

Dawn on Wednesday found me at the stand where my camera had photographed the 5-pointer. The wind was okay but not perfect, but it would have to do. Imagine my surprise when two does and two fawns wandered by at mid-morning, the very first deer I had seen all week! This occurrence wasn't enough to keep me in the woods beyond Wednesday, but it did buoy my spirits somewhat.

The rest of the morning and early afternoon were quiet. A couple of ruffed grouse entertained me. First, they landed in trees around my ground blind, clucked to each other for a while, and then one took off and crashed into the side of the blind, just about causing me to jump out of it. That bird fluttered into a nearby tree, clucked its embarrassment to its buddies, and then flew through my shooting lane with the others following shortly.

When the grouse left, I looked ahead to a potential two-hour window between moonset at 3:55 p.m. and sunset at 5:51 p.m., hoping something good might happen.

It didn't take long.

My trail camera recorded it at 4:03 that afternoon when the odd-racked 5-point buck stepped into my shooting lane. Instantly I brought my muzzleloader up, found the buck's rib cage in the scope, pulled back the hammer and squeezed the trigger. Through the smoke I watched the buck lurch forward and then run off and disappear. The highlight of the hunt was over in less time than it takes to tell its story.

I reloaded my muzzleloader, dug my GPS from my pack (in case the tracking job would prove longer than I thought), made sure I had my tag, gut knife and rope, and climbed out of the blind.

Curiously, there was no hair, blood or other sign of a hit where the buck stood, and for a moment I remained in the spot and puzzled over it. But then I looked in the direction the buck had run and saw a piece of lung lying on brown leaves, and smiled. "Got him," I said to myself.

The blood trail started about 15 yards from where the buck had stood. First it was just a splash of bright blood, but

then it became such that I just walked along with only an occasional glance down at the trail. I found the buck lying just
over a rise, piled up into a fallen, long-dead jackpine, its eye
fixed and staring skyward. I knelt and gave thanks, musing at
how quickly my hunt had turned from one of desperation to
joy. I pulled the buck from the dead branches, ran my fingers
over his unusual antlers, and then cut the appropriate slits in
the tag and zip-tied it to the antlers.

The next day I kept my promise to my wife and returned
home, only the trip was more enjoyable due to the buck lying
in the bed of my truck. I knew he wouldn't weigh 200 pounds
dressed but would be close, and when I hung him in my
garage he pulled the scale to 185 pounds.

We all want to kill a giant buck every time we step in the
woods, especially when on a special hunt to which you have
looked forward all year. But given the sometimes-tenuous existence the northern whitetail lives, you have to be happy with
what's available. I've hunted northwoods bucks for a long time

A front-end photo of the author's buck shows how unusual its rack was.

and have seen what winter can do to deer herds, but prior to the 2013 season I had never before witnessed the kind of damage that the previous winter had caused. The 5-point buck was the largest that my cameras recorded over a 3-week period at several proven deer stands, and I have to be satisfied with that.

FURTHER NOTES ON THE 2013 HUNT

The full extent of the winter of 2012-13 wasn't known until after the final season closed in the northwoods, yet its impact was one that few who are attuned to such things will ever forget.

Hunters in many locations reported that the top-end bucks were simply gone, and the few that remained had smaller antlers than what they had carried in previous years, or their antlers were deformed in some way. Trail cameras provide an accurate assessment of the deer herd and many hunters reported a complete lack of big buck pictures.

At my hunting camp, trail cameras placed before the sea-

The author with his odd-racked 5-pointer.

son produced no photos of bucks older than what were likely 2½-year-olds. In fact, we had more pictures of spike bucks than bucks with forked antlers, and several of the spikes did not meet the 3-inch requirement for a "legal" buck. I saw two of these animals while hunting — they appeared to have pencil stubs sticking from their foreheads.

In one northern Wisconsin county, biologists who aged deer found that more than 80 percent of the 1½-year-old bucks registered by gun-hunters had spikes for antlers. What's even more astonishing is that a high percentage of the 2½-year-old bucks registered at the same stations had spike antlers.

The winter even extended its fingers into some of the agricultural southern counties in Wisconsin and Minnesota. In some locations, the older bucks that hunters had pursued for years had vanished. A friend who experienced this at his hunting land noted how there were about 80 deer bedding on an open hillside while he was setting up turkey stands in April. "We would drive by them in the UTV, and if they even got up at all, they would just stand up and watch. Once we passed,

A sub-legal spike buck photographed by the author's trail camera in northern Wisconsin in 2013.

they would bed down again. They were that stressed," he said.

Another friend who hunts private land where Quality Deer Management is practiced intensively shot a giant 6½-year-old 8-point buck, but found its antlers were considerably smaller than its sheds from the previous season.

It wasn't all gloom and doom, because my trail cameras revealed some places where the bucks came through the winter in decent shape. Where I live, backyard feeding is very prevalent. My cameras at my bow-hunting stands photographed more big bucks than the cameras I had placed near my hunting camp and at my out-of-state hunt location combined!

To make matters worse, as I finish this book the record-setting winter of 2013-14 is just coming to an end. Many weather stations in the northwoods are calling it the coldest and snowiest winter on record. Deep snow limits deer movement and buries much of their food, so they can't replenish the calories they burned surviving the bitter cold. It is a certainty the northwoods will lose deer but how many remains to be seen. Coupled with the previous winter, northwoods hunters may see difficult times until the herd rebounds.

As a hunter, it's sad and frustrating to see what severe winter weather can do to our beloved white-tailed deer. It's a fact of life the northwoods deer hunter must accept because there's really nothing we can do about it but hope for better days in the future.

Incredibly, the issue of hunter access has extended its troublesome fingers into the northwoods.

THE FUTURE OF NORTHWOODS HUNTING

It would seem there are battles being waged against the northwoods white-tailed deer, or at least the hunting of northwoods deer.

More than 30 years ago, conservationists with great foresight warned that hunting in North America could one day become a "rich man's sport," as in Europe, where only those who own or lease land may hunt. I scoffed at this idea because, not only do the northern tier of states have tremendous acreage of national, state, and county forest land, but millions of acres of land owned by timber interests were also available to hunters. I reasoned that no matter what happened, hunters could always find somewhere to go.

But that has changed. With the current state of the paper industry, the beancounters of the paper-making companies have figured it is more cost-effective — and more profitable for their shareholders — to sell their holdings and buy the rights to log the land of private landowners. Each year, increasing numbers of hunters are finding the timber company land they may have used for generations is no longer open to them because it's either been leased by someone else or sold outright.

Of possibly greater concern is the threat of public land being sold to private interests. This idea has been floated by legislators looking to balance budgets. While long-term wisdom has so far held sway over short-term political gain, I worry for the future. Thirty years ago I could not imagine "industrial" land being sold off. Will the same happen to public land in another 30 years?

The increasing fractionalization of private lands produces further pressure on the northwoods hunters' way of life. As the value of large private holdings increases, the desire and ability of the succession of owners to keep the acreage intact diminish. While this could be a good thing, meaning that more hunters may now be using lands that previously were open to only a few, not everyone who buys the parcels may hunt or even approve of hunting. Roads are built and homes pop up, and their construction and presence alter deer habitat, the animals' movements, and how we hunt.

Thankfully, a vast majority of the non-hunting public has remained level-headed enough to approve of hunting, but this could change. While big antlers appeal to all of us, the non-hunting public — including those who may be the neighbors of our hunting land — must understand the primal needs of the hunter are important, too. They need to see us as other than a bunch of trophy-minded savages; rather, we feel a need to gather as friends and families, and hunt to provide meat for the table. Hunters need to portray a positive image of what we do so the opinions of non-hunters are not influenced by the few knuckleheads among us, or by the animal rights group whose stated purpose is to do away with our hunting traditions.

As non-hunters take to the woods, they are also taking positions within state wildlife agencies. Gone are the days when a hunting background was required, or was at least a foot in the door, for employment. The decisions that affect our time in the woods are often being made — or at least influenced — by people who have no knowledge of hunting outside of what they may have read in a textbook or on the Internet.

We see this already in the decisions being made by state agencies with regard to predators. While having a population of predators is always a good thing for overall deer herd health (and needs to be supported by hunters) the overabundance of predators in the Great Lakes and Western states as of this writing is severely impacting deer numbers.

True, state agencies were handcuffed by Endangered Species Act protection of timber wolves and the lawsuits brought by animal rights groups that followed efforts to delist them. However, when these same agencies continue to over-protect other predators like black bears and bobcats — when their own research data indicates more of the animals could be harvested without harming their overall population — one has to wonder who is calling the shots and why.

The debate over timber wolves is the loudest at this writing. In Wisconsin, we have always had bears, coyotes and

A trail camera captured this image of three wolves eating a buck's entrails less than four hours after it was shot.

Stealth Cam   044 F   10-26-2011 16:32:24

bobcats, and with wolves being the new kid on the block they are taking the most blame, warranted or not. I wonder if wolves aren't experiencing what biologists call "exotic vigor," in that a species that is new to the local environment overwhelms it initially before finding its niche. The fact that wolves have always been present in Canada yet do not seem to have any appreciable effect on the daily movements of deer, leads me to believe we may see wolves become just another critter on the landscape sometime in the future. I hope this is the case someday.

State agencies are also increasingly under the influence of legislators whose opinions and backgrounds often have no business in (what should be) the objective world of wildlife management ... yet there they are.

Hunters need to support logging because this is in the best interest of the deer herd. Deer eat just about anything except that which they cannot reach, and as forests mature, deer vanish. The idea that as trees are cut they are replaced by concrete and asphalt is largely wrong, for timber is a renewable resource. Sterile, old-growth forests limit the plant types that can grow in their shade, and support few wildlife species because of a lack of food. Cut the timber, let sunlight reach the forest floor, and watch what happens. As young trees sprout, so do the deer. A large variety of species, whether plant or animal, is true biodiversity.

Older forests combined with high predator numbers have severely limited the northwoods deer herd's ability to bounce back after long, cold winters. Previously, the deer herd would quickly rebound when biologists reduced or eliminated antlerless tags for a couple years following a bad winter. Not so now.

Hunters also need to be supportive of one another. Too often hunters have the petty viewpoint that "If I can't or don't want to do that, you shouldn't be able to, either." The arguments — length of bow-hunting seasons, crossbows, antler point restrictions, traditional vs. modern muzzleloaders, baiting, antlerless tags, etc., can seem endless on Internet forums and in the letters to the editor sections of hunting magazines and local newspapers. I have always been of a more accepting nature, believing that we should not limit opportunity if it does not harm the resource or create safety concerns. It's a slippery slope when people try to regulate the ethics of others.

Caught in the middle is the poor state wildlife biologist, or game manager as some prefer to be called, who walks a tightrope of trying to do what is right for the resource while all of the issues mentioned here are threatening to pull him into the abyss. As more than one has told me privately, "If all I had to do was manage deer, my job would be easy because they will do just fine on their own. It's the people management that is difficult."

Managing northwoods whitetails really doesn't have to be that hard. Biologists had it figured out long ago when someone said, "To manage deer, all you need do is feed them popple in summer and lead in the fall." Translated, this means if we provide proper habitat and keep their numbers in check through hunting, the deer herd will be just fine.

Complicating the management of the northern whitetail is man's desire to see them, either in their backyard or on their privately-held hunting property. In some places, backyard feeding has become so prevalent that deer no longer go to "deer yards" to spend the winter, but hang out on the edge of people's backyards.

Backyard feeding and food plots on private land create hotspots where deer numbers are often much higher than public land, where the majority of the hunting takes place.

Game managers issue tags for antlerless deer to be taken because all signs point to a deer herd that needs thinning, but then the tags get used in the places (public land) where the deer herd often needs to be increased. At this writing, it appears Wisconsin will soon issue separate antlerless tags for private or public land. Whether this will happen and then make a difference remains to be seen.

We are taking steps in a positive direction in one very important statistic — hunter numbers. New data at this writing indicates the population of hunters in rising, and the biggest increase is in the number of young females entering the sport. This is a very good thing.

So, how does the northwoods deer hunter survive? Somehow, we need to keep large, unbroken tracts of public forest intact because, after all, it is the wilderness that has drawn most of us to hunt it in the first place. We need more logging to keep food available for the deer we hope to hunt. We need

The author took this doe from private land where deer trails go from one backyard feeder to another. The situation has created an unusually high deer herd in the neighborhood.

predator numbers that are better balanced with what our deer herds can tolerate, and/or what humans will tolerate. And we need to be more respectful of the desires of other hunters, and of the efforts of those who are working for us.

Thoughtful hunters are needed in these debates. If we work together we can overcome the challenges in front of us. This wonderful heritage of northwoods deer hunting demands that we keep it going for future generations.

THE AUTHOR

Steve Heiting has long been known as an outdoor writer and editor. He sold his first article to *Outdoor Life* magazine in 1985, and in 1991 was named editor of *Wisconsin Outdoor Journal* magazine. He joined *Musky Hunter* magazine in 1994 as its managing editor, a position he holds to this day.

Steve also serves as a contributing writer to *Wisconsin Outdoor News*, for which he writes about a dozen hunting and fishing articles each year. His articles and photographs have appeared in more than two dozen magazines and newspapers covering the outdoor sports.

Hunting Northwoods Bucks is Steve's third book. His first, *Musky Mastery*, is considered a classic in the sport. Steve also teamed with Jim Saric to write *The Complete Guide To Musky Hunting*. He has written, edited or contributed to 20 books about musky fishing, and has produced five instructional musky fishing DVDs.

Before his career turned to the magazine business, Steve was a newspaper editor for nine years, winning multiple awards from the Wisconsin Newspaper Association.

Steve and his wife, Connie, live near Minocqua, Wisconsin. For more about Steve, visit www.steveheiting.com or www.muskyhunter.com.